THE CHILDREN'S MEDIA YEARBOOK 2024

The Children's Media
FOUNDATION

The Children's Media Yearbook is a publication of The Children's Media Foundation

Director, Greg Childs

Administrator, Jacqui Wells

The Children's Media Foundation

15 Briarbank Rd

London

W13 0HH

info@thechildrensmediafoundation.org

First published 2024

© Hannie Kirkham, Laura Sinclair and Dr Ashley Woodfall for editorial material and selection

© Individual authors and contributors for their contributions

All rights reserved. No part of this publication may be reproduced, stored in a retrieval system, or transmitted, in any form or by any means, without the prior permission in writing of The Children's Media Foundation, or as expressly permitted by law, or under terms agreed with the appropriate reprographics rights organisation. You must not circulate this book in any other binding or cover.

Cover and book design by Rebekkah Hughes

ISBN 978-1-9161353-6-9

Contents

Editors' Foreword — 5
Hannie Kirkham, Laura Sinclair & Dr Ashley Woodfall

The Children's Media Foundation: Chair's Report — 6
Anna Home OBE

The Route To The Summit – And Beyond — 10
Greg Childs OBE

A View From The Summit: A Report From The Children's Media Summit 2024 — 13
Dr Greg Boardman

Raising The Nation: How To Build A Better Future For Our Children (And Everyone Else) — 16
Paul Lindley OBE

Bagpuss, Dear Bagpuss, Old Fat Furry Cat-puss — 20
Chris Tichborne

Revolutionising The Broadcasting Landscape: The BFI Children's 'Gamechangers' — 24
Professor Máire Messenger Davies

Dick And Dom's 'Bogies': A Shout Out For The Irreverent — 28
Dr Ashley Woodfall & Professor Richard Berger

Harnessing A Creative Audience: Dubit's 25th Anniversary — 33
David Kleeman

100 Years Of BBC School Broadcasting — 36
Dr Steven Barclay

BBC Children's & Education: Why Do We Care? — 40
Patricia Hidalgo

Why Edutainment Matters — 44
Ahrani Logan & Sam Harris

Legacy Of YACF: Two And A Half Years Later — 48
Jackie Edwards

The State Of Children's TV In The UK — 51
Di Redmond

Young Voices And Content Classification: The Future Of Age Ratings — 54
Dr Chris Davies & Dr Wallis Seaton

The UK's Local Television Network: A Hidden Gem In The Public Broadcasting Landscape For Young Audiences? — 58
Jill Hurst

It's Africa's Time — 62
Steve Rock

Larrikins And Lighthouses: A Time Of Change In Australian Children's Television — 65
Dr Liam Burke & Dr Joanna McIntyre

Children's Television For Intercultural Dialogue: *La Lleva* — 69
Dr Enrique Uribe-Jongbloed

***Pocoyó* As A Spanish–British Cultural Milestone** — 71
Silvia Rusiñol Romero

The Power Of Representation: Children Who Migrate *Jana Navarria, Makaela Lewis & Zoë Speekenbrink*	74
Can We Normalise Children's Rights Through Children's Media? *Professor Dawn Watkins*	79
Paying Attention: Is Toddler Attention Shaped By Early Media Exposure? *Professor Tim Smith, Professor Rachael Bedford, Claire Essex & Dr Hannah Pickard*	81
Rethinking Short-Form Media For Generation Alpha *Dr Sonia Tiwari*	85
Putting Children's Wellbeing At The Centre Of Digital Play Design *Dr Fiona Scott*	88
Anonymous Apps: *Gossip Girl* For The Platform Generation *Dr Ysabel Gerrard*	92
Social Media, Kidinfluencers And The Changing Discourse On Childhood *Dr Jane O'Connor*	95
***Cosmic Kids Yoga*: From Birthday Parties To Apps And Beyond!** *Jaime Amor*	98
Sport Will Save Us *Maurice Wheeler*	102
Think And Wonder, Wonder And Think: Children And Philosophy *Sally Latham*	105
Playful Storytelling To Inspire Oracy *Lucy Walters*	110
For The Love Of Play! From Ragdoll To *Mixmups* *Karen Newell*	112
Something Old, Something New: First Forays Into Children's TV *Chitra Soundar*	115
Remembering Ursula Von Zallinger *David Kleeman*	119
Remembering Kay Benbow *Alison Stewart*	121

Editors' Foreword

Hannie Kirkham, Research and Strategy Manager, Oriel Square, **Laura Sinclair**, Doctoral Researcher, School of Journalism, Media and Culture, Cardiff University and **Dr Ashley Woodfall**, Associate Professor in Children's Media, Bournemouth University

It's another bumper edition of the *Yearbook*, as we air the key debates within our field – and this year we are pleased to welcome Laura Sinclair, from Cardiff University, to the Editorial Team. Croeso!

Children's media is in a state of uncertainty, with problematic policy and funding challenges at play. We can't avoid discussing some of these issues, but we also look to highlight some positives and possibilities, for both those working within children's media and children themselves. Digital platforms and emerging technologies continue to give us many opportunities to engage with children in new and exciting ways. Young audiences continue to embrace digital media, gaining agency and bringing their voices to the fore. But that is sometimes at the expense of the established safety nets of 'traditional' media. Optimistic notes need tempering when we turn to ethical and safety issues, and the challenges of keeping up with progress.

The *Yearbook* features articles written by people who are creatives, policy makers and researchers, all with one thing in common – their clear (and at times nostalgic) passion for children's media. This edition truly showcases how we all keep childhood alive in the media we create for our own children and the children around us, how we encourage and protect them, but also where we fall down as an industry – grazing not just our own knees.

We start with discussion on this year's *Children's Media Summit*, which grappled with young audiences' migration from public service to digital content. We move on to the history of children's media and how game changing programmes have created a legacy that embodies the interplay of childhood, inner childhood and being grown up. We also take an international tour, looking at perspectives and experiences from Australia, Colombia, Spain and across Africa, as well as look at how our home media can talk to the realities of displaced families' and migrant children's lives and stories on screen.

There is plenty more insightful, intriguing and occasionally challenging discussion across the *Yearbook* – as we span play, apps, edutainment, influencers, children's development and rights, yoga, sport and philosophy – for starters! Diolch yn fawr.

The Children's Media Foundation: Chair's Report

Anna Home OBE, Chair, The Children's Media Foundation

In the 2023 *Yearbook* we highlighted concerns about the long term future of public service media for children following the closure of the Young Audiences Content Fund, and the failure of future regulation for children's content in the Media Bill that had just started its journey through parliament.

In the months since, the Children's Media Foundation (CMF) has devoted a great deal of time and effort to addressing these issues, culminating in the Children's Media Summit held in London on 28th February 2024. Significant progress has been made, but as CMF Director, Greg Childs, will explain in his report (see page 10), much still remains to be done. However, although the Summit has dominated the Foundation's work this year, there has been plenty of activity in other areas.

The executive group, chaired by Alison Stewart, has grown and now has 26 members, each with their own specific area of work. All members of the group are volunteers, and we thank them because we couldn't do without them. The areas they cover range from issues of diversity and inclusion to research liaison, digital and broadcasting policy, event management, editing the *Yearbook*, industry liaison, communications and more.

The industry liaison group has developed a new activity this year: regular, informal, monthly online 'get togethers' hosted by group members. Special guests from the children's media industry and associated areas are invited to share their knowledge and experiences. This is proving to be a good way of meeting new people, exchanging information, ideas and concerns, and debating potential solutions.

Organising events remains an important part of the executive group's role and these might be discussions around policy issues or simply entertaining evenings. For example, in September 2023, at the 'What's Happening to Kids TV' all-party parliamentary group (APPG) meeting in the House of Lords, chaired by Baroness Benjamin, Sky Kids set out their position and ideas, answered questions and joined the discussion with industry guests. We plan more of these meetings as they are a good way of keeping up with what the various broadcasters and platforms are planning for the future and bringing them to the attention of parliamentarians and invited industry guests. In the future these will not be happening as part of a formal APPG, due to new more complicated administrative rules on APPGs imposed by parliament. Instead, Baroness Benjamin has agreed to continue to host parliamentary meetings in a less formal way.

Other events in the autumn included the CMF QuizNite held at – and generously supported by –

legal firm, Lee and Thompson. It was hosted by comedian Tiernan Douieb and the questions were set by Tom Jordan, who does a similar job for *Mastermind*!

It was much enjoyed and proved to be a useful fundraiser. As always fundraising remains a major concern. CMF relies on supporters, patrons, and corporate funders to keep us going. We realise that times are hard but please join us if you can as every donation counts. In the last 12 months we have been lucky enough to welcome two new Lifetime Patrons – CBeebies presenter Chris Jarvis and the multi-talented Sharna Jackson both joined and we are hugely grateful for their donations.

CMF will continue its event programme at the Children's Media Conference in July 2024. We will be responsible for the editorial guidance of three key sessions: the opening *Question Time*, which is always hugely popular, the closing *CMC Debate* (this year inevitably a follow up to the Summit), and a new session on the ethics of AI interfacing with kids, which is an area of special interest to us – and we have started work on liaising with academics considering the ethical issues.

Other partnerships are thriving. The Children's Coalition, led by Baroness Kidron's 5 Rights Foundation, continues its work as the Online Safety Act becomes law and responsibility passes to Ofcom to regulate against online harms. The Coalition is keeping up pressure to ensure that the principles enshrined in the Act are carried forward to the regulatory process, and has sent a detailed outline of what is needed to ensure the law is enforced with vigour.

CMF is also a member of the Public Service Media Forum founded by the Voice of the Listener and Viewer (VLV). We were extremely honoured to receive a VLV award in November 2023 in recognition of CMF's services to Children's Broadcasting. We're equally pleased to continue as active members of the Forum, which campaigned for changes in the Media Bill to ensure that certain genres like religion, arts and science are designated public service media priorities. Children's, like News, *is* already listed as a priority in the Bill, but we remain concerned for the other public service genres too. What is the point of providing for children's public service content if there is no guarantee of public service range and choice in the programmes they see when they become adults?

The inclusion of children in the "protected genres" in the Bill might be seen as positive, but in reality it is ineffectual: the Bill fails to regulate shared video services like YouTube or TikTok, where so much of the children's and youth audience has migrated. The proposed regulation is not suitably future focused and certainly does not address the massive changes that have already taken place in the younger audience.

This is our focus going forward: a new public service compact – fit for the 21st Century – and persuading those in power to give these new ideas full consideration.

Finally, I would like to pay tribute on behalf of CMF, to Kay Benbow who sadly died in March this year. She was a passionate defender of quality content, especially for the younger age groups, and her period as Controller of CBeebies was one of great achievement, innovation, and success. Kay was a keen supporter of the foundation from the very beginning. We remember her with gratitude and affection.

The Route To The Summit – And Beyond

Greg Childs OBE, Director, The Children's Media Foundation

The Children's Media Summit on February 28th 2024 was a major milestone for the Children's Media Foundation (CMF), for the media industry in the UK and, we hope, for children and young people.

The Summit was a meeting of some of the key organisations that advocate for the young audience, as well as representatives of the people who make and distribute media for them. It agreed a statement that outlined the most pressing issues facing the audience and industry – specifically, the significant migration of the 7+ audience away from broadcast services to shared video platforms such as YouTube and TikTok. This affects not only the wellbeing of young people but has societal and cultural implications. It also threatens their loyalty to public service media in the future.

Basically – how can we expect people who have never benefited from public service content to want to watch or pay for it when they get older?

The Summit statement also outlined a set of potential solutions to be put to the government to alleviate the situation – for the benefit of the audience, society and the kids' media industry.

Greg Boardman was at the Summit for CMF and outlines his view of the day's proceedings and outcomes in his article on page 13.

I'd like to reflect on the journey CMF took to reach the Summit – and what we think should happen next.

It's been a long march, that's for sure. Ofcom has been surveying the children's audience and industry for 20 years. As viewing figures (and therefore advertising revenue) declined and the commercial public service broadcasters commissioned less content, the regulator declared 'market failure' in the children's sector. The BBC increasingly took on the role of sole provider. In 2019 the arrival of the Young Audiences Content Fund and its distribution of £44m of development and production finance over its three-year pilot provided some relief. New series were commissioned and made by the commercial PSBs. But apart from preschool content – where the audience is still watching channels like CBeebies or Channel 5's Milkshake! – programmes for older children and teenagers did not reach their audiences.

In 2020 CMF Deputy Director Colin Ward led the publication of a multi-authored report: *Our Children's Future – Does Public Service Media Matter?* Innovative articles by leading figures in television and media-watchers with new ideas about funding and support for public service media, set the agenda for the work ahead. The report crystallised thinking at CMF, and led to new members joining the Board and the formation of a policy group that would address the actions needed to make change.

CMF staged a series of public events to debate the ideas expressed in the report and to explore potential solutions. This began with 'Show Me the Money' in 2021 and continued with an evaluation of the Young Audiences Content Fund after its closure, followed by the more urgently titled 'Sleepwalking over the Edge' in 2023.

At successive Children's Media Conferences from 2020, CMF produced debates that pushed the issues higher up the industry agenda. This has raised industry awareness of the strategic and long term nature of the changes taking place.

The final part of the strategy grew from one of those CMC debates in 2022, when the Director of Children's and Education at the BBC, Patricia Hidalgo, asked to meet the contributors and CMF representatives to discuss the issue of audience flight to YouTube and TikTok and the strain on public service provision this creates.

Patricia's support led to CMF bringing the issues into the political sphere through a series of meetings of the All-Party Parliamentary Group for Children's Media and the Arts (APPG), chaired by Baroness Benjamin and attended by industry leaders. The commercial PSBs, the BBC and Sky all had their days in parliament and they were remarkably honest about the problems they faced, offering ideas for solutions – including, in the case of the BBC, a new idea of enhanced tax incentives to stimulate culturally relevant programming. All the participants seemed keen to take things further with Ofcom and the politicians, who would make the final decisions about the future of public service content for children and young people.

This, then, was the route to the Summit. After the 2023 CMC debate 'Public Service RIP?' the clamour to *get something done* was loud and clear.

The CMF immediately began work on an event to bring all the interested parties to the table. Over the autumn the key stakeholders attended an unprecedented series of meetings to discuss the way forward. The BBC, ITV, Channel 5, Channel 4, Sky, Pact, Animation UK and the campaign group, UK Children's Media Plan, spent nine hours openly discussing the lost audience, the lack of culturally relevant content and how that might worsen the 'crisis of childhood'.

The meetings also debated a range of possible solutions and, although not all were accepted unanimously, a useful list was created covering funding, regulation and what will need to change to make public service fit for the future.

All of this was then discussed at the Summit at the end of February 2024. The large event, which took place at the BFI in London, included producers, broadcasters, YouTube and YouTube makers, academics and children's advocates – many of whom expressed concerns about the value of public service content no longer reaching young people.

As a result of the Summit process, the Children's Media Foundation has come to the conclusion that radical change is needed. We need to accept that the audience has flown – and may well fly again to new platforms and new activities. But this doesn't mean that the concept of public service content for young people needs to wither on the vine. We need instead to consider how to renew the public service relationship on the platforms where children do watch.

The Summit declaration has, since February, been used to brief government ministers, civil servants, Ofcom, the Labour Party front bench and the Liberal Democrats. It is now very firmly in the public space – exactly as the Summit intended.

The Media Bill does not address the issues highlighted at the Summit. The changes apply to the broadcasters' online delivery of their content – on platforms that young people are not using any more. The new regulations are largely irrelevant for the audience over the age of seven.

However, the Summit briefing document did stimulate a number of amendment proposals that sought to add a 'postscript' to the Bill to guarantee a special investigation into the state of the children's media market in the UK and how that affects the audience.

It has been satisfying for CMF to hear praise from all parties in parliamentary debates for our work to bring this to public attention and to offer up a series of possible solutions. As this article reflects – it's been a long road from 'crying in the wilderness' to broad general acceptance that something needs to be done.

Now our job is to maintain the momentum and follow through with:

- the new government – whatever the shape of the Media Bill – on the principle that this can be a major contributor to young people's wellbeing
- Ofcom, who have assured CMF that their 2025 review of public service media in general will feature significant learnings from the children's and youth sector and their recent children's survey
- YouTube and other new platforms, as we try to persuade them that the time has come – across the world – to take a pro-social stance; to find ways to surface culturally relevant, age appropriate content that has depth and meaning for young people, rather than the endless algorithmic doom scroll of the most watched content; and that they could consider partnerships with public service providers that not only ensure their content is seen but reward producers for it.

Funding and *finding* are now our keywords – to inform the industry campaign and politicians who are seriously considering change. We hope in the long term they will open the doors to a better media life for our young people and better opportunities for the children's media industry in the UK.

A View From The Summit:
A Report From The Children's Media Summit 2024

 **Dr Greg Boardman**, Producer, Composer, Musician and Writer

Having been involved in the pre-Summit discussions and debates it was with mild apprehension that I arrived at BFI Southbank to participate in what was billed as a unique coming together of stakeholders. Realistically, given the mountainous problems being forced upon us by the digital world, this summit could only be the first peak, a foothill on the way to steeper and more challenging climbs. As I put pen to paper, businesses responsible for wonderful creations are going bust. We are a sector looking for urgent solutions. Like many colleagues I carry a heavy burden, concerns about the futures of the companies I work for and the skilled people who make the magic happen. However, by far the heaviest burden I carry is the deep concern for the young people who represent the future of our communities. The diverging needs of business and public service apply opposing forces that add yet more weight to the load, though in the current political climate I am encouraged to measure value in purely monetary terms.

At the start of the Summit day, demanding optimism, Paul Lindley struck a wonderful tone by quoting Nelson Mandela as he reminded us that children are "our future" and represent our "greatest asset". A positive attitude seems essential if we are going to apply our collective expertise to develop short and long term solutions, but we also need the political establishment to recognise the significance of *hearing* the voices of youth: be warned, just being seen to listen is not enough. Without doubt we are dealing with a crisis of childhood, but we should recognise that it is not the children themselves who are the crisis but the systems we have allowed to envelop our young people. Put another way, we must accept responsibility for the problems that have surfaced on our watch. In turn the establishment ought to recognise that the talents within our sector are more than capable of developing solutions if empowered to do so. Afterall, children's producers have been at the forefront of funding issues for decades and innovation has emerged from those challenges.

To strike a balance between the needs of our businesses and the voice of youth we must adopt an ethical approach. This isn't a choice, a woke option, it is enshrined in the United Nations Convention on the Rights of the Child, an obligation on all professionals working with young people. However, can we say that we are taking an ethical approach when, to paraphrase Maddie

Moate, dominant digital infrastructures are 'optimised' to collect data and clicks rather than focusing on the audience or the quality of *their* experience? Surely it is no longer good enough for society to adhere to the notion of adulthood starting at the age of 18 while turning a blind eye to big tech following their own rules and declaring the end of childhood at the age of 13. Why are we in such a rush to hurry our young people into adult consumers?

The analysts and media researchers, armed with their slides, graphs and pie charts, provided a stark reminder of what we all knew before we arrived. That said, what might have been news to many at the Summit was the revelation of how broken the systems of measurement are when it comes to the screen habits of young people. We might count clicks and swipes and hours of engagement, but we can't know if we are doing what is best for the child. Inspired by the data, we might be tempted to blindly follow the mantra of putting the content "where the audience is"; superficially it makes sense. On the other hand, we might reflect on David Kleeman's observation that the younger generation has been bequeathed with no "frame of reference" in the choices they make when self-curating their digital world. New tech frequently boasts about the power to manipulate habits of behaviour; this drives their models of investment. But when it comes to creating high quality, culturally relevant content the data lays bare just how little we invest in producing public service content that will create positive lifelong habits amongst our young. It might be suggested that we are experiencing a blip, a byproduct of a severe global downturn, but Kate O'Connor left no doubt that funding for children's genres is contrary to other adult-focused genres where increased investment is very evident over time. Given that four times as many children access content through YouTube's main app as opposed to YouTube Kids, it seems, for the most part, that we are happy to throw our children into the deep ocean without even giving them a basic swimming lesson. The open sea is full of wonderful and diverse things but there are plenty of sharks lurking, ready to bite.

We might unanimously agree on the fact we have a crisis in the systems around childhood. Though as expected, when it comes to conversations about funding, next steps, the short term fixes and the long term planning, despite a desire to speak with a unified voice, tensions, conflicts and discrepancies between the broadcasters and stakeholders emerge. Levies, quotas, obligations, tax credits, licence fees, direct government funding; every solution has positives and negatives, proponents or detractors. This is no surprise and a feature of any marketplace, especially one suffering the turbulence of market failure. But ask yourself, if we put the audience first, is it okay for us to conceive of the children's media space as a market? Our digital world offers *some* young people access to myriad opportunities but there are substantial numbers of families who are *not* thriving, with children suffering a lack of diversity of experience. The marketplace that has evolved is one of inequality where access to content is not equitable, whichever way one chooses to approach the notion of access. Magnus Brook stressed that unlocking funding is only useful if we can actually get the public service content in front of the relevant audience once it is produced. We have to explore the intricate relationship between funding and finding while avoiding knee-jerk reactions. No one funding solution is going to satisfy the traditional channels, content producers and the new mediators of content. However, this lack of agreement about solutions might provide a couple of valuable takeaways. Some traditional channels of delivery may need to retire gracefully, handing back the privileges that come with public service. And, if no one funding solution will suffice then we can also agree that no one entity can be relied upon to deliver to and engage with our communities. I can't believe that anyone would argue against plurality and diversity within our content. So, maybe plurality and diversity within the funding sphere is a key to an inclusive world of tech and media, all the while remembering that the child must come first. Furthermore, letting go of traditional avenues of engagement should not automatically lead to a reliance or dependence on emergent channels of engagement that put commerce before community.

Drawing on the sentiments of Gary Pope, who spoke from the Summit floor, it might be sensible to accept that any and all content is public service content, if it is made for the attention of children. Do we then develop this notion to stress that any medium or platform aspiring to deliver a public service should accept that children represent a quarter of the audience? We should be in no doubt that professionals across our sector, along with parents, must take responsibility, being brave, curious and forceful as we regulate for good quality and culturally relevant content with the same vigour we might regulate for online harms. Producers attending the Summit were encouraged to prioritise YouTube as part of their strategies, embracing low-budget or no-budget production to compete with unregulated, user-generated content. Unfortunately, this feels like our wider society burying its head in the sand. Simply put, if channels want to engage with young audiences and lay claim to serving the public then they ought to share the risk by funding quality content and not force producers to bear the upfront costs.

Ultimately, we are dealing with a political problem and one that needs the attention of our government and the treasury, now and in the future. Realistically, only qualitative data gathered over many years will ultimately provide a summative assessment of our actions and achievements. 40 plus years ago (on *Why Don't You?*) we were challenged to switch off our televisions to go and do something less boring instead – a wonderful notion with some truth at its heart – but that was in a day where the channels actually switched themselves off. Today we have been guided into a realm where apparently content must be available 24/7 putting huge strains on the pathways of childhood and teenage development.

What is very clear is that inaction is not an option for anyone working in the children's media space. The next steps will not be a solo climb for a single agent, nor can it be a dash to a safer plain for our well-funded corporations. This first Summit marks a beginning, a chance to build on Paul Lindley's optimism to bring our community into a new and exciting space. I am grateful that the key stakeholders shared their thoughts, their hopes and fears. I, in turn, hope that we will continue to pull together as we take on the difficult next ascent.

Raising The Nation: How To Build A Better Future For Our Children (And Everyone Else)

Paul Lindley OBE, former Nickelodeon executive, founder of Ella's Kitchen, Sesame Workshop Trustee and Chancellor of the University of Reading

This article is based on Paul's keynote speech from the Children's Media Summit 2024.

30 years ago, applying for a job at Nickelodeon, I was so excited by the possibility of working in children's television. Since then, I've worked in, on or around children's issues, trying to nurture and empower children to get off to the best start on their perilous but exciting journey to adulthood. At that exact time, Nelson Mandela gave a speech that deeply affected me, and still does now. It set my purpose in life and the personal journey I have since travelled. He said: "there can be no keener revelation of a society's soul than the way in which it treats its children…" going on to add "Our children are the rock on which our future will be built. Our greatest asset as a nation."

With those words ringing in my ears, I got that job at Nickelodeon and spent nine wonderful years there before leaving to start Ella's Kitchen, which became the UK's biggest children's and baby food brand. I'm now a trustee of the Sesame Workshop, I also chaired London's Child Obesity Taskforce for four years, and am now the Chancellor of the University of Reading.

Those 30 years saw great optimism for building a nation where all childhoods are important and all are supported: we had a government that took over one million children out of poverty, the hope that the technological revolution brought and new media opportunities for education, entertainment and social connection. Over the past decade the focus on children first stalled, and then went into reverse, regarding their wellbeing, welfare and opportunities. This was because of government priorities, economic policies and political choice. But also the cultural deserts that a globalised youth culture, technological developments and ineffective regulation have created.

During the pandemic, when children suffered the harshest lifelong impacts from lockdowns (remember that pubs opened before schools) I thought deeply about Mandela's words, their impact on me, and the seed he had sown all those years before. Sustained by its hope, and my continued belief in the importance of a child-centred future, I began researching and writing my book Raising the Nation – How to Build a Better Future for Our Children (and Everyone Else) (2023). It challenges us to redefine what success looks like for a society and is a draft manifesto for what a big public policy framework and ideas could look like *if* we prioritised a commitment to ensure every child has the chance to feel significant, to have a thriving childhood and to become the person that each has the potential to be.

I *do* believe we have a fundamental crisis of childhood in this country today. It is born from four basic ways childhoods have transformed over the last generation. First of all – everyone under 30 has grown up in a volatile, uncertain, complex and ambiguous (VUCA) world, where planning a future is impossible and stress is toxic. Throughout their lives, they have experienced one national or global crisis followed by another followed by another, be that environment, social justice, austerity, public health, personal health, technology, terrorism or geo-politics. Second, their lives have been lived in a world where short-termism dominates institutional decisions like never before, in business (the rise of private equity), education (the rise of league tables and SATS), politics (populism, and the mythical promises of 'oven-ready' solutions) or the media (24 hour news cycles and ubiquitous social media). Third, the digital revolution has changed every aspect of childhood, from the positives of offering connections, knowledge and belonging, to the negatives of content, contact, conduct and consumer risks. Finally, children make up a significantly smaller proportion of our overall population than they did when I was born, yet even though our GDP has doubled, they are more than twice as likely to live in poverty. Our society is now incredibly more diverse but our public services have not adapted to be relevant, reflect fairness or give equality of opportunity across all childhoods. And that includes public service children's media.

Not all children thrive today; too many have no voice to shape their lives. They get stuck in systems that don't hear their lived experiences or true needs. Too many don't have a variety of positive experiences in childhood, by which to be inspired for their purpose, their passions, the things they are good at, their confidence and drive, their tolerances and empathy. And too many don't have their wellbeing measured, prioritised or protected: be that at home, at school, in the public space or online.

We see how this fails our children by the facts, for example, that 40% of London's children live with an unhealthy weight and one in six children has been diagnosed with a mental health issue – an increase of 60% in the last three years. Half of all youth centres have been closed in the last decade, and over 500 playgrounds since 2016. We see it in the way that the social media companies feel it is perfectly OK to define a 13 year old as an adult to push content and algorithms and collect their data, yet in their terms and conditions highlight that some of such content may be harmful to those under 18. Yet *we* allow this. What does this reveal about our society's soul?

A key ingredient in a nourishing, stimulating childhood is high quality, freely available and culturally relevant drama, information, entertainment, edutainment and storytelling content. These ingredients are critical for children to understand who they are, get a true perspective of their environment and of the culture and heritage of their individual communities within the society in which they are growing up.

Children are not a 'minority' in society. Everyone is or has been a child, and the role of public service children's TV in fostering curiosity, encouraging literacy and inspiring citizenship has long been regarded as public service TV's key contribution to post-war generations. Public service, or socially beneficial, media can:

- help a child understand their town, their country and their world
- develop understanding, valuing and ownership of, what it means to be British
- create a will to engage, participate and contribute to society
- provide role models, inspire ambition and encourage social inclusion
- engage young people in national conversations that drive them to participate as adults in the future.

If anyone is in any doubt about this, just consider the importance to you of the role models children's television gave you and their encouragement of your ambitions. For decades, healthy competition between public service broadcasters, within a well-regulated framework, meant that UK children's broadcasting was the envy of the world and exported everywhere as a key signal of British values and 'soft power'. It's maybe no coincidence that from 1945 until the 1970s inequalities of opportunity lessened and social provision for children and families increased. High quality, freely available, culturally relevant television for children played its part in that landscape. But this world has gone by. Broadcast TV now accounts for about 15% of 6–11 year olds screentime – only three years ago it was more than 35%. Ofcom estimates that less than half of 3–17 year olds now watch live television.

Instead, many children now find their media content on video-sharing platforms that are aimed at international audiences and dominated by US content. They also have to navigate the pressures and complexities of adult-focused media without the support of public service content tailored to their needs. Who do we want our children's role models to be? Is it the influencers or extremists on social media, or is it the diverse and inclusive performers and characters we see on public service children's television?

> "High quality British children's content will become scarce and could become extinct. Parents, politicians and producers need to step up before it's too late."

I'm not suggesting we can turn back the clock to a cosy world of *Watch with Mother* and nice people on *Blue Peter* – nor am I suggesting that the past was wonderful and the present is scary and nasty. But I do think it is vital that children's content helps to give children more voice, a variety of positive experiences and protects their wellbeing in the decades ahead. Today's children have more choice and easier access to storytelling and information than any of us ever did as a child. But how they find accurate information and culturally relevant inspiration is down to the whim of huge, largely unregulated international corporations. And the decreasing amount of high quality British content for kids is hidden in a quagmire of – at best dubious, and at worst dangerous – stuff.

Regulation is generally to prevent harm – what about regulating to promote good? To break down inequalities, build up inclusion and expand horizons of opportunity. We also generally regulate the amount of children's content broadcasters *produce*. Is it time to set quotas for how much content is *consumed*? What would incentivise public service broadcasters and others to ensure 'nourishing' content reaches the audience, wherever they now are, and be incorporated into the algorithms that push content? What of the streamers and video sharing platforms, that currently are largely free of obligation when it comes to offering quality content for British children, yet *can* be regulated and brought 'inside the tent' as we have seen with the impact of the Age Appropriate Design Code and the Online Safety Act? What's the quid pro quo from the wealthy companies who dominate our children's viewing?

In the US, *Sesame Street* has led the way in creating public service children's television, and then innovating to remain relevant and vital to children's wellbeing as the media landscape has changed. They've moved from helping disadvantaged kids learn ABCs and 123s in the 1970s, to helping children process emotions like grief and anxiety in the 1980s and 90s, to providing humanitarian responses for displaced children, helping children see autism as an opportunity to be inclusive, and now to creating 'Sesame Street in Communities' content, off broadcast TV, to support children and families with specific issues like opioid addiction or incarceration. The ensuing strategy to deliver this mission has involved re-looking at its revenue streams, content focuses and diversification in both distribution and content.

The ideas put forward in my book, *Raising the Nation*, include ensuring that Arts are seen as a necessity, not a luxury, and offering schools the opportunity, capacity and resources to put creativity at the centre of their teaching and learning systems. How could public service children's content play a part in this classroom transformation? Can this sector develop Kitemarks for best practice, incentives to reach it, or tax credits for those organisations that illustrate content changes in their products informed by the principle of children thriving? Can public service children's media find an indispensable role in a National Play Strategy, be that broadcast, on demand or received through social media, that could help childhoods thrive in the context of the UK and British culture and environments? I think it can; I think it must.

We are at a moment of inflection. Decisions, policies and regulations made today will have impact for a generation or more as we cross the Rubicon to a digital, platform agnostic, future for children's media. This industry can play a leading role in helping children thrive in this world. But you'll need to be brave, curious, creative, innovative, entrepreneurial and forceful, to make the case to, and partner with, the government and set the agenda for building a better future for our children and, therefore, everyone else. We *must* involve children in defining our challenge, exploring solutions and understanding why they make their choices.

High quality British children's content will become scarce and could become extinct. Parents, politicians and producers all need to step up before it's too late. As well as our great tradition of making high quality British media for children, we risk losing our heritage of growing new producers and writers. Once the traditional, regulated broadcasters and their budgets are no longer being found by children, who will pay for this vital element of our children's nourishment?

Bagpuss, Dear Bagpuss, Old Fat Furry Cat-puss

Chris Tichborne, Director of Animation

"Bagpuss, dear Bagpuss, old fat furry cat-puss." Those were the poetic opening lines as we saw a Victorian style, sepia photograph of a sleeping Bagpuss transition into a full colour animated film.

Today in 2024, as we celebrate 50 years of this Smallfilms classic and reflect on the continuing appeal of this iconic series, I want to look at some of the facets that made this show unique and how it resonated with me far beyond my childhood.

Was it the peaceful co-existence of characters of all shapes and sizes from different backgrounds who worked together to solve the mystery of an unknown object? Many observers have commented on all sorts of connotations and political undertones of Oliver Postgate's work, but the biggest impression on me as a child was to see real life objects come to life. This was my epiphany that eventually led me to a career in stop-motion animation.

Oliver Postgate and Peter Firmin made 13 episodes of *Bagpuss* for the BBC that aired from February 1974 (the year of the tiger!) and were regularly repeated until 1986.

Sandra Kerr's folk-inspired musical compositions and performance were the perfect complements to the aesthetics and sensibilities of the show. The first few notes of the opening theme tune offered a feeling of safety and comfort and felt like an antidote to the noise and busy-ness of other programmes aired at a similar time. Kerr's soundtrack took us back to a time of England's past and the use of classic instruments to create mystical sound effects ensured a timelessness to the music and the show.

Using the stop-motion technique, Bagpuss came to life with a big yawn. For me, the moment of transition between a static sepia monochrome picture to animation in colour was reminiscent of the moment when Dorothy walked through the door into the glorious Land of Oz. The visual transformation of time and place transported me into a magical environment that I could relate to. I could almost smell the scent of old wood, leather and lacquer from the north London antique shops that my parents would take me to as a child. They too were cluttered with trinkets, toys and ornaments that held secrets to the past. I remember several times turning my head quickly to see if I could catch something moving on a shelf behind me.

In the history of storytelling, we have seen many toys and objects coming to life. *Winnie the Pooh* and *Pinocchio* are good examples, and more recently we see them going undetected by humans in *Toy Story* or *The Lego Movie*, where fantasy mirrors reality. The inhabitants of 'Bagpuss & Co.', the shop in which *Bagpuss* is set, come alive and are sentient for a very short period between long sleeps. Every episode begins with the same visual narrative in the form of a photomontage as Emily delivers a newly found object. Her magic words would wake Bagpuss and his friends, but she would be gone by the time they had surfaced from their slumber.

Bagpuss & Co. was more of a lost property department than a shop. As a child, it was perfectly plausible for these altruistic establishments to exist amongst an emerging backdrop of capitalism and consumerism. After all, from an early age, we were taught about the merits of honesty and charity. Towards the end of each episode, the busy mice would push the found item to the shop window in the hope that its owner may notice it in passing. Who knows if the rightful owners would eventually reclaim their lost property, but it made me consider all those many people in the world who may be missing something or even someone.

This was a show where rescued objects hypothesised and reflected on the provenance of other recently found items. It formed an interesting formula for endless entertaining possibilities. Oliver Postgate had previously, in 1969, tackled this idea with *Clangers*. Those woolly, whistling creatures would discover objects that landed on their home planet and we would watch how they interacted with them.

This theme of intrigue, sparked by unknown objects and the mystery of their origin, may have resonated with my young self as I tried to make sense of the new surroundings in my world. Sometimes, I would instantly recognise what the object was that Bagpuss and friends were trying to interpret. For this, it may have given me a clue to how people arrive at conclusions about things without formal evidence. Perhaps Postgate's fertile imagination and humour reflects the absurdity of our own evaluations to reach conclusions that are purely hypothetical.

Each character's personality would bring different perspectives and curious assumptions to the discussion on the found item. Professor Yaffle, the wooden bookend woodpecker would be the first to discover the newly placed object. His dry, objective analysis and academic pomposity would lead the conversation. Bagpuss would take

Professor Yaffle, Madeleine and Gabriel

this further down the rabbit hole of myths and legends based on his curious past life. This added to the mystery of how our cloth cat ended up in the shop in the first place. How did such a well-travelled feline end up in lost property?

Madeleine the rag doll and Gabriel the cloth toad were fixtures who were locked to their bases. To me, this gave them a sense of authority – they didn't have to rush down to join the huddle. I have worked in animation for a while now and I can see that this may have also been purely for practical and technical reasons. Postgate was known for filming up to two minutes of animation a day, which in comparison to today's studio output is nothing short of heroic. Each animator on a modern-day series will be expected to shoot up to 12 seconds a day. Although we have the technology to produce a more fluid movement, I can understand the pace at which Postgate must have been working to achieve such a prolific output. He wasn't shy about using live-action shots to speed up the process too. When Gabriel sang and played his banjo, Postgate shot it in real time as it was puppeteered from below the set using Firmin's specially designed rig. This added another dimension to the character. He became more alive than anyone else!

In 2014, I got to meet and work with Peter Firmin on the new series of *Clangers*. He was generous with his anecdotes from the Smallfilms days when they filmed in the converted pig shed next to his house in Blean, Kent. He was a brilliant artist, printmaker and problem solver who was always looking for objects that he could use or adapt for props and sets. When he brought the original Iron Chicken to the studio, he pulled out a Swiss Army Knife from his back pocket and

Chris with Emily Firmin and Bagpuss

started to tighten the tension on its legs! To me this demonstrated Peter's practical approach that a puppet was still a tool, and that this famous artefact from television history was still capable of doing the job it was intended to do.

Smallfilms was very much a family affair – without the intrusion of external 'experts' and advisers. Perhaps this lack of committee allowed them to experiment and pioneer the techniques that made *Bagpuss* so unique. Peter's wife, Joan, who was a professional bookbinder, made many of the beautiful puppets for their shows. Even their children were given practical tasks to help with the fabrication.

Firmin's stories of the events and settings that led to the creation of *Bagpuss* made it sound like they were very much flying by the seat of their pants. His humble and matter-of-fact descriptions can't disguise the reality that he and Postgate were visionaries whose genius could sometimes be guided by fate and instinct. For example, there's the 'happy accident' story about why Bagpuss is pink. Peter explained how he had placed an order for marmalade coloured fur. Somehow, the fabric company in Folkestone mixed up the order and dyed it pink by mistake. Peter's decision to embrace this turn of fate to create something truly unique was typical of his artistry and quick thinking.

The nation's affection for our iconic candy-striped moggy is still very much alive. In 2018, we filmed an episode of *Clangers* where a human astronaut (based on Dame Maggie Aderin-Pocock) visits their home planet. As we prepared for the shoot, I found an opportunity to sneak a little nod to *Bagpuss* in the film. When the astronaut pulls out her keys to her rocket door, we got a close-up shot of a *Bagpuss* keyring made by the props department. We presented the episode to a large audience at Bluedot Festival at Jodrell Bank in 2019 to celebrate the 50th anniversary of the show. As the close-up shot of the keyring appeared on screen, a huge sigh of affection and a cheer resonated from the crowd. It's always interesting to watch films with an audience because their reaction allows you to gain an insight to how it may be received by the rest of the nation. This particular moment said all the right things.

A group of us were lucky to join Peter at the 2015 BAFTA awards. He was to receive a Children's Special Award that evening and I found myself sitting next to his daughter Emily at the ceremony. As we settled at the table, she produced a bag from under the table. With a cheeky grin, she pulled out the Bagpuss puppet! It was a pinch-me moment when she handed him to me. I was lost for words and felt instantly transformed back to a ten year old boy. The thrill of sitting in the company of Bagpuss and the girl in the sepia photographs reminded me of many of the reasons why I chose a career in animation and children's television. Yes, I'm just a big kid and I know it.

Those early stories and characters become part of the fabric of our lives. *Bagpuss* should remind us that we don't always need fast paced, super-slick productions with an intended 'educational message' bolted to the script. Good stories, kindness and inclusivity with well-rounded characters are a good start. We should look back to Smallfilms as a benchmark of all these things as we continue to develop shows for our future adults.

Revolutionising The Broadcasting Landscape: The BFI Children's 'Gamechangers'

Dr Máire Messenger Davies, Emerita Professor of Media Studies and Policy, Ulster University

Earlier this year, in February, the Children's Media Foundation (CMF) launched a campaign, 'Responding to the Crisis of Childhood', asserting:

> "We believe today's children's audience should be given access to the same range of culturally relevant, trusted and life-affirming content that was made available to previous generations, in a form and on platforms that reflect the way children and young people live today."

This is an ongoing theme for the CMF. In last year's edition of the *Children's Media Yearbook*, Joe Godwin, a former head of BBC Children's, asked: "Does public service content for children still matter? … Our knowledge, experience and instincts tell us that high quality, culturally relevant storytelling for children is one of our most precious cultural assets".

How do we recognise a 'high quality' piece of work, when trying to persuade policy makers that this material is worth preserving and worth continuing to produce? What examples can we use to illustrate our case? Some academics have been concerned about this lack of critical attention to specific examples of children's programmes, comparing it to the much greater critical attention given to children's literature. Little has changed since children's media researcher David Buckingham wrote in 2002:

> "While there has been an enormous amount of research on children as an audience, critical discussion of media texts that are specifically designed for them has been severely lacking… While children's literature is now a relatively legitimate topic for academic work, children's media is not." (*Small Screens: Television for Children*, p11)

This contrast is a point Anna Home, CMF Chair and another former head of BBC Children's, has repeatedly made. Of course, many writers and industry researchers have written about specific children's programming over the years since 2002 – IZI (the International Central Institute for Youth and Educational Television), who organise the PRIX JEUNESSE, is a special case in point. (See their special edition of Televizion on quality from 2009.) And there are the BAFTA awards in the UK every year. Some academics have noted that there's some interesting quality material out there, for instance, Anna Potter on the current worldwide hit, *Bluey*. But, given the crisis in children's media production, which at the Children's Media Summit conference was presented as part of a wider crisis of childhood, it seems important that policy makers should have their attention drawn to what we might be losing.

Why do I care? Over the years, I have actively enjoyed watching children's television with my own four children, now all grown-up, and my three grandchildren, finding it often more entertaining and innovative than much adult television. It was thanks to children's television that I began my career in this field by reviewing children's programming for *The Listener* magazine in the 1980s. So, for me, it was good news when, in 2022, celebrating the BBC's 100th anniversary, the BFI produced a list of what they called 100 gamechanging BBC programmes, and that 12 of this hundred – a remarkably high 12 per cent for a 'minority' audience – were children's programmes. I was particularly interested in the language used for justifying the BFI's choices. In what sense were these programmes 'gamechanging'? Were the criteria the same for children's programmes as for adults'?

It's worth reminding ourselves of why it matters that the BFI, a publicly funded institution, founded in 1933, with a statutory duty to preserve the UK's audiovisual heritage, should pay attention to children's programming, at a time when it is under threat. Their mission is:

- to support creativity and actively seek out the next generation of UK storytellers
- to grow and care for the BFI National Archive, the world's largest film and television archive
- to offer the widest range of UK and international moving image culture through our programmes and festivals – delivered online and in venue
- to use our knowledge to educate and deepen public appreciation and understanding of film and the moving image
- to work with government and industry to ensure the continued growth of the UK's screen industries (www.BFI.org.uk).

These are the BFI's 12 choices of gamechanging children's programmes.

- *The Sooty Show* (1955–1992)
- *Blue Peter* (1958–)
- *Vision On* (1964–1976)
- *Play School* (1964–1988)
- *Camberwick Green* (1966)
- *Newsround* (1972–)
- *The Multicoloured Swap Shop* (1976–1982)
- *Grange Hill* (1978–2008)
- *Teletubbies* (1997–)
- *Something Special* (2003–)
- *Horrible Histories* (2009–)
- *Bitesize Daily* (2020)

Sooty and Sweep

This is how they introduced their 100 choices:

> "These are the shows that revolutionised the broadcasting landscape by defining and developing entire genres; here is the creative talent that broke ground to represent diverse communities across the UK in new and meaningful ways; these are the programmes whose impact changed social attitudes by challenging the status quo; and the technological landmarks that shaped how we watch television today… Guiding all of our thinking was the need to represent the remarkable range of the BBC's programming… music shows like *Top of the Pops*, pioneering current affairs programmes such as *Panorama*, and, of course, the BBC's essential programming for children, from *Sooty* to *Something Special*."

This seems to me to be a helpful way of looking at the quality of children's programmes – locating them in the television ecology of the time. They don't make any qualitative distinction between adults and children's programmes in terms of their originality and influence on future developments. There's no separate list for children's, the programmes are listed chronologically, which leads to some interesting juxtapositions. For instance, *The Multicoloured Swap Shop* (1976–1982) was number 54, sandwiched between *I, Claudius* (1976) with its 'diabolical DNA', and *Pennies from Heaven* (1978) – 'a quantum leap forward' in original drama. A similar revolutionary spirit is attributed to *Swap Shop*. According to the BFI: "Nothing as edgy, exciting and unexpected as all this had been done on national television before […] *Swap Shop*'s influence can be sensed, if not always seen, in every slightly uncertain live-and-dangerous Saturday morning kids' series that has come since."

I was surprised to see *Camberwick Green* (1966) described as 'revolutionary'. The very first article I ever wrote about children's television, for *The Listener*, was called 'Feudalism for the under-fives', about the show's odd mixture of modernity and squirearchy. But the BFI writers point to a key factor in children's TV, particularly the preschool genre that *Camberwick Green* embodied: 'world building', that enables the 'wealth of merchandising' on which subsequent developments of preschool 'worlds' now financially depend. They point out:

> "Freddie Phillips' music and the voice of *Play School* favourite Brian Cant helped build a world that was bursting at the seams, leading to the follow-up series of *Trumpton* (1967) and *Chigley* (1969), and a wealth of merchandising that was a sign of things to come."

Further examples of their definitions of 'gamechanging' and 'creative talent that broke new ground' come in their descriptions of *Vision On* (1964–1976):

> "Segments ranged from simple stop-frame animation to state-of-the-art computer graphics and included some mesmerising, almost psychedelic visual experiments… Kids TV has continued this visual, non-verbal approach in series such as *Something Special* and many others, making it inclusive not only of deaf children but of those for whom English is not their first language."

They point out that *Newsround* (1972–) – at number 48, sandwiched between *Mastermind*, 'an unapologetic celebration of specialist knowledge' and *The Family*, 'the roots of reality TV?' – was a training ground for eminent adult journalists: 'its alumni of staff is an impressive list of reporters and newsreaders, who often cut their journalistic teeth on *Newsround*, including Helen Rollason, Krishnan Guru-Murthy, Lizo Mzimba and Matthew Price'. A similar 'seedbed' for adults', in this case, comedy writers, performers and actors, has been *Horrible Histories* (2009–): 'The cast and writers have become a regular troupe, expanding their comedy to other series, including *Yonderland* (2013–2016), *Ghosts* (2019) and a feature film about Shakespeare, *Bill* (2015).'

Given the term 'gamechanging', the primary criterion of inclusion in this list is 'how it changed television', that is, the programme's influence on other shows and on society more broadly – its afterlife and legacy. This is children's television as a seedbed, generating the early careers of writers, such as Frank Cottrell-Boyce and Russell T. Davies (*Grange Hill*); directors and producers (Anthony Minghella and Phil Redmond, also *Grange Hill*); comedians, writers and actors (the *Horrible Histories* team). Then there are journalists (*Newsround* again) and politicians (Floella Benjamin, *Play School*). These examples all worked in children's television and brought the skills and experiences gained there into their later careers.

The BFI list argues the case for the material's cultural importance, using terms like visionary; pioneering; interactive; groundbreaking; inclusive; creative; anarchic; generating new adult shows and performers; technologically experimental and innovative. Many key creatives started their careers in children's television and are now shaping the cultural world of the rest of us. It has been a seedbed of talent and – yes – revolution. In, say, ten years' time, will the BFI or any other organisation be able to point to the current generation of UK produced children's material and say: this was groundbreaking; visionary; revolutionary, inclusive, interactive, technologically innovative? This is a question for us all to address now. We need to pay serious critical attention to the quality of children's media and to learn from, and pay tribute to, what has gone before.

References

100 BBC TV Gamechangers. https://www.bfi.org.uk/lists/100-bbc-tv-gamechangers

Buckingham, D. 2002. *Small Screens: Television for Children.* Leicester University Press

Potter, A. 2020. Globalising the local in children's television for the post-network era: How Disney+ and BBC Studios helped Bluey the Australian cattle dog jump the national fence. In: *International Journal of Cultural Studies.* 24(2). https://journals.sagepub.com/doi/full/10.1177/1367877920941869

Mikos, L. 2009. Quality is a Matter of Perspective. In: *Televizion*. https://izi.br.de/english/publication/televizion/22_2009_E/mikos.pdf

Dick And Dom's 'Bogies':
A Shout Out For The Irreverent

Dr Ashley Woodfall, Associate Professor in Children's Media and **Dr Richard Berger**, Professor in Media & Education

The UK has had a rich history of genuinely irreverent and at times radical children's television. Some of these shows have been extremely subversive, with many challenging the practices and structures of the adult world. In this light we will consider Saturday morning live children's television, spanning the era from *Tiswas* (1974–82) to *Dick and Dom in da Bungalow* (2002–06), with a particular focus on the later show's 'Bogies' pre-recorded inserts.

Children's television has often sat at the centre of highly contested debates about what constitutes 'childhood', and clumsy 'media causes harm' debates have positioned children's TV as a bad influence and responsible for poor behaviour. Shows as recent as *Teletubbies* (1997–2001; 2015–18), *Pokémon* (1997–), *Rastamouse* (2011–15) and *Peppa Pig* (2004–) have all been criticised at times for their seemingly malevolent grip on their young audience. As we shall see, *Dick and Dom in da Bungalow* similarly faced criticism for being a bad influence and in poor taste.[1]

Dick and Dom in da Bungalow ran for 263 episodes and was first aired on the then newly-launched CBBC channel, scheduled against other live studio based shows *SMTV Live* (1998–2003) on ITV and *The Saturday Show* (2001–03) on BBC One, before *da Bungalow* itself moved on to BBC One in 2003. As was common to other children's Saturday morning shows, *da Bungalow*'s 'zoo format' combined live studio segments with pre-recorded inserts, with one of the inserts, 'Bogies', acting as a playful 'prank' disruptor of public space 'acceptable behaviour'. 'Bogies' followed *da Bungalow*'s two presenters, Dick (Richard McCourt) and Dom (Dominic Wood), as they, tentatively to start, competed with each other to 'hijack' places where etiquette and behaviour aligned with conventional (serious and humourless) adult social norms – such as museums, libraries, theatres, restaurants and even a yoga class.

Children's television, as we generally recognise it, is inherently made by adults *for* children, with little room for children's genuine input into a production. However, Saturday morning children's TV in the UK almost always featured a rowdy live audience, with children taking part in quizzes,

---

[1] Julia Day, '"Lavatorial" Dick and Dom Criticised in Parliament', *The Guardian*, 18 January 2005. <https://www.theguardian.com/media/2005/jan/18/broadcasting.bbc>

activities and even interviewing celebrities and popstars. In this way, children could be seen as claiming some measure of agency and even, at times, acting as 'co-owners' of the show. Yet this agency was generally limited to 'playing along' with the intent of the producers and presenters (not independent of it), and the children within the audience didn't get to bring much of their 'real' lived experience to the screen.

On *Dick and Dom in Da Bungalow*, the two adult presenters performed as exaggerated character versions of themselves. This exaggeration was sometimes extreme, such as when performing as mini cupboard-bound 'Diddy Dick and Diddy Dom' characters. For most of the time on screen, they could be seen to perform as the 'children's TV presenters' Dick and Dom, rather than as their 'authentic' Richard and Dominic selves. Adopting a 'child-like' persona, they operated in studio within a world shaped *for* children (by the producers of the show), and, keeping this childlike persona in play, they then re-entered, and disrupted, the 'adult world'. 'Bogies' featured Dick and Dom in hybrid 'constructed' settings, as they inserted a pre-shaped scenario into seemingly real situations. Here we should be cautious as to how much control of the 'real' environment might have been in the hands of the production team, and this caution should also be applied to the 'reality' of the challenges as presented on-screen in relation to shot choices and edit decisions. Most 'Bogies' end with Dick and Dom 'fleeing the scene' like criminals and then dissolving into laughter during a post-challenge debrief and replay. During this post-mortem the double act look back on the experience, both as themselves and as if they were the audience. The in-challenge (often repressed) laughter translated into a post-challenge release, as they act as audience for themselves and in turn as proxy for the child audience.

Dick and Dom sit within a 'double act' tradition that spans comedy and children's television. The Chuckle Brothers' show *ChuckleVision* (1987–2009) brought a Laurel and Hardy-like comedy to children's TV, but their double act was traditionally scripted and allowed little room for interaction or improvisation with the audience. Trever and Simon's comedy sketches on Saturday children's television shows *Going Live* (1987–93) and *Live and Kicking* (1993–97) did offer room for interaction with children, but here the comedians remained in character. However, it was Ant and Dec who can be said to have established a successful children's TV double act template. Ant (Anthony McPartlin) and Dec (Declan Donnelly), originally child actors, had mastered their double act during their time presenting *SMTV Live* (1998–2003), switching between performing as themselves and in character. With the turn of the millennium however, they were successfully relocating their enthusiasm, playfulness and soft irreverence to primetime TV; they had left a 'gap in the market' for others, like Dick and Dom, to follow.

Dick and Dom, and in particular the 'Bogies' challenge, can also be seen to be shaped by the work of comedian Sasha Baron Cohen in his Ali G and Borat personas, both of which were significant in the cultural landscape at the time *Dick and Dom in da Bungalow* first aired in 2002. The 'in da' within the show's title acts as a direct homage to the *Ali G Indahouse* film of the same year. As Sasha Baron Cohen stated, the 'discoveries' within Ali G and Borat were the 'idea of taking a comic character into a real

situation',² and that 'an Establishment setting was a wonderful place to prick pomposity and undermine it'.³ This coupling of character/real hybridity with the ways in which Ali G and Borat would routinely subvert the hubris or arrogance of those representing established knowledge and authority, also play out, in a less provocative manner, within 'Bogies'.

Many UK children's TV shows can be seen to be irreverent and, to an extent, radical; showing a lack of respect for people or institutions that are otherwise taken seriously. Looking at *Tiswas*, for example, a 'running order' led rather than scripted show, we see presenters like Lenny Henry, Chris Tarrant and Jasper Carrott, who had strong backgrounds (and futures) in adult comedy, slipping in and out of character. The show, first aired in 1974 and produced by ATV for the commercial ITV network, can be seen as a counterpoint to the safer shows on the BBC. *Tiswas* featured irreverent characters and sketches, and often children were more than just a distant, passive and approving audience; they were seen to play along with the sketches and 'lean into the frame' as presenters sat amongst them, rather than in front of them. Intriguingly, it may be more than coincidence that *Tiswas*, the earliest of the shows discussed so far, aired across a time when punk was born and became a defining cultural force.

Prior to *Tiswas*, presenters and characters would interact with children appearing on shows in limited ways. The children might be cheering, on cue, within the audience; be a contestant on a show like *Crackerjack* (1955–2020), the BBC's long-running children's gameshow; and they might occasionally appear as callers, vetted and rehearsed by a researcher to ensure they hit the right 'marks'. Yet within these confines, there are moments where children didn't behave as intended (for example, when the pop group, Fivestar, were abused during a live phone-in on *Going Live*). In general however, the child on-screen could be seen to be a safe contained proxy for the actual child audience, representing a socially ideal child, rather than children in themselves with their own agency and voice.

Saturday morning children's television was, of course, made by adults, for children, but these shows tended to be live, loosely scripted and usually featured children not just in the audience, but as participants too; controlled

---

² Sasha Baron Cohen, 'Sacha Baron Cohen: The Man Behind the Mustache', *Rolling Stone*, November 30, 2006. <https://www.rollingstone.com/tv-movies/tv-movie-news/sacha-baron-cohen-the-man-behind-the-mustache-249359/>
³ Sasha Baron Cohen, 'Sacha Baron Cohen: "The idea is to give up all my undercover work now"', *British GQ*, 4 September 2021. <https://www.gq-magazine.co.uk/culture/article/sacha-baron-cohen-interview-2021>

Screengrabs taken from YouTube

chaos was the order of the day. The shows appeared at times obsessed with bodily functions (often farting) and food: particularly interaction with food, and food-like substances, in ways that would not be acceptable in other settings – and indeed, in an Ofcom ruling in 2012 on one of Dick and Dom's follow up shows, the UK media regulator identified concern for the wellbeing of child participants during a 'vile concoction' in-studio eating challenge. *Tiswas* famously featured the (custard pie throwing) 'Phantom Flan Flinger' with many shows ending in some kind of food fight. *Tiswas* also helped cement the children's television 'gunge' tradition of covering child contestants, and adult 'guests', in a slimy-runny custard. *Dick and Dom in da Bungalow*, although operating in a different broadcast era, was little different. The show routinely featured contestants and hosts being covered in gunge and what Dick and Dom dubbed 'creamy muck muck'.

'Bogies' itself featured Dick and Dom entering often 'sacred' adult spaces, such as museums and libraries. Once there, they would act like children – or how children would perhaps like to behave. Dick and Dom would then take it in turns to say or shout the word 'Bogies' at increasing levels of volume until one conceded defeat – the challenge being won by the presenter who shouted or screamed the loudest – with embarrassment seeming to prevent the loser from continuing. Hidden cameras would capture reactions to hearing the shouts and each challenge would be edited together with an innuendo-laden voiceover, in a mock sports commentator style: it's a "battle between two giants of the game" (in a cinema), it's "very, very tight at this stage of the game" and "is the pressure starting to show?" (in library settings).

During the 'Bogies' challenge at the Mitchell Library in Glasgow the presenters are immersed in the 'hushed' traditions of the old-fashioned reference library. The library users we see are all adults and appear to be using the place for silent reading and study. It is unlikely that many, or any, of the library's users have an awareness of the double act or the 'Bogies' rules of engagement. Dick and Dom look like they might be of student age, so the challenge could appear to be a student prank of sorts and a few younger library users appear amused by the shouts, but the shaken heads and stern scowls of the older library users seem to articulate a clear annoyance at the ways in which Dick and Dom are breaching formal library etiquette. The double act's own highly repressed laughter suggests a significant discomfort within the library environment – and it is notable that the 'Bogies' shouts at the Mitchell Library feel the most muted and awkward within the challenges overall (only reaching a '4.2' on the show's on-screen graphic audio level 'Bogie-o-meter', compared with a full-throated '9.6' at the International Boat Show). The subversion of behavioural norms is of course only temporary, and arguably the awkwardness, and in turn the comedy within these challenges sits in the tensions inherent between the subversion and normal order being reasserted.

Over time the structure and conventions of 'Bogies' became more established and understood by the audience – and during the challenge set in a cinema, they begin to join in; with some children by the end on their feet screaming 'Bogies!', much to the obvious embarrassment of many adults around them. During a challenge similarly set within a live theatrical performance of *Peter Pan*, an actor on the stage opens with: "All children grow up…" and the voiceover immediately adds: "… apart from Dick and Dom!". The children in the audience clearly get the 'joke' and sense what is happening as the volume of 'Bogies' increases – the adults do not, and broadly remain contained within the conventions of being in a theatrical audience (however pantomime-like). Within this specific 'Bogies' the children perhaps become as much part of the performance and experience as the actors on the stage.

Unsurprisingly, perhaps, *da Bungalow* tended to upset those who prefer a certain behaviour from children on- (and off-) screen, and there were even calls in the UK parliament for the show to be taken off-air for being 'lavatorial', with MP Peter Luff asking if the show is 'really the stuff of public service broadcasting'. However, debates about the appropriateness of the content on children's television, and *Dick and Dom in da Bungalow* specifically, might be recognised as more about a 'fear of childhood' than any serious concerns about harm.

Production of *Dick and Dom in da Bungalow* concluded in 2006, bringing to an end the era of live, loosely scripted Saturday morning children's television (*The Saturday Show* having ended in 2005). The spirit of these shows does live on, to a much lesser extent, in some corners of children's TV. Notably, live studio links (between programmes), such as Hacker T. Dog's chaotic, and often quite adult, appearances on CBBC, have long offered space for playful subversion, but with the decline of the main channel children's TV programming, and in turn the decline of the children's standalone channels (with children's offerings moving towards on-demand and online) there is less and less space for the irreverence that had once been a significant part of UK children's television culture.

The generation that grew up watching *Dick and Dom in da Bungalow* are now young adults, but the children who followed, growing up in a streaming and social media era, are of course no less irrelevant. Indeed, content made *by* children is now common and shared through platforms like YouTube and TikTok. Although there are routine fears for children's wellbeing in relation to these platforms and the media on them (whether made by or for children), they do offer children agency, and agency to be irreverent and radical, in ways that traditional children's TV, made *for* children, never fully could.

You can find the full discussion from Dr Ashley Woodfall and Dr Richard Berger in the forthcoming book Radical Children's TV (Edinburgh University Press).

Harnessing A Creative Audience:
Dubit's 25th Anniversary

David Kleeman, SVP Global Trends, Dubit

As Dubit celebrates its 25th anniversary, we've been reflecting on the seismic changes we've witnessed in the media landscape. When Dubit was founded in 1999, its record-setting young board of directors wanted to give youth a voice in the social gathering spots that were emerging online.

At the time, the internet was a very different place – limited to words on digital web pages like blogs and listservs. Social platforms like MySpace were still four years off, and YouTube – representing video-based second-generation UGC – was six years in the future.

Dubit was officially launched by then Secretary of State for Trade & Industry, Patricia Hewitt

Over the subsequent quarter-century, falling distribution costs and revolutionary creative tools have fueled three massive waves of user-generated content (UGC), each reshaping the industry in profound ways. Now, as we look ahead, we believe the next wave – driven by platforms like Roblox – will be the most disruptive yet.

The first UGC wave was text. Open-source software and early social platforms like MySpace put publishing power in the hands of regular users. Print media scrambled to adapt as audiences fragmented.

The second wave was video. Smartphones enabled anyone to record, edit and share video. YouTube and other similar platforms exploded in popularity, taking away the monopoly on consumer attention from traditional curated and scheduled television. If you had a camera and something to say, you could find an audience.

25 years later, following many twists and turns, Dubit is still in the business of virtual worlds, but in the transformative third generation of UGC. Now, ever-improving tools enable nearly anyone, anywhere to build and share multi-dimensional spaces that blend text, video and explorable games and experiences. These worlds are immersive and interactive social spaces, complete with customizable avatars, virtual clothing and tools, and a thriving digital economy.

It's not hard to envision the factors that will shape Dubit's (and the media world's) next 25 years. Artificial Intelligence (AI) will enable even more people to bring their creative visions to life. Today's platforms will form a more coherent 'metaverse' with social, play, learning and commerce elements that parallel and connect with real life. The power to create and distribute content will decentralize media, empowering communities to collaborate directly without gatekeepers.

Having watched previous waves upend the media landscape, we at Dubit are convinced that the UGC 3D revolution will be the most disruptive yet, rippling far beyond gaming to reshape social interaction, commerce and creative expression.

For established media players, this presents both existential threats and incredible opportunities. Trying to compete head-on with the volume, variety and fast-evolving nature of UGC is a losing game. Instead, the future will belong to those who find ways to enhance UGC, to provide complementary curated experiences, and to harness user creativity.

Below, Dubit co-founders **Ian Douthwaite** *and* **Matthew Warneford** *talk about what's changed, what hasn't, and what lies ahead for innovators in immersive media.*

Dubit got its start building virtual worlds, and 25 years later it's building new kinds of virtual worlds, in Roblox. Talk a little about the differences in possibilities then and now.

Ian Douthwaite (ID): We never actually stopped building virtual worlds, because games and edtech need a coherent narrative and structure in order to be engaging and 'sticky'. We built a world called 'Kart Kingdom' on the PBS Kids website, where young people designed their own karts to travel around and join with others in games that were often collaborative. By connecting the games in virtual space, it encouraged kids to explore more deeply than a set of standalone activities.

But, it's true that the rise of mobile tablets and smartphones, and the growth of UGC video on YouTube and other platforms, shifted people's focus and time to individual apps.

Matthew Warneford (MW): Every new wave of engagement has been made possible by software and hardware advancements that make new forms of creation more accessible and more affordable, and facilitate broader distribution. In doing so, they disrupt the existing methods.

The immersive worlds we're able to create today rest on increasingly powerful design engines that enable deep 3D spaces to explore and interact, high-capacity multiplayer servers so players' engagement can be social, and the UGC tools that put the power of creation in everyone's hands.

Today, people live deep and active lives on immersive platforms – they play, socialize, learn, create, shop and more. What was the main attraction for users of virtual worlds in 1999?

ID: At Dubit, we often quote Jeff Bezos' that many people ask him what is going to change in the future; few ask what won't change, which he sees as more important. There really isn't any change in people's motivation for playing, learning and socializing in virtual spaces; what's evolved is the depth, scope and richness of the experience.

For example, the power to create experiences, and the extensive ability to customize spaces and avatars, enables young people to use virtual worlds for self-expression in new ways. They try on personas with virtual clothing, represent their favorite brands, and create around their fandoms and passions in UGC spaces.

How has the growth of UGC platforms changed the process of hiring for a games studio like Dubit?

MW: The tools for world-building are mostly free. They're easy to learn, so anyone can get started, but they're robust enough to enable almost limitless possibilities. The young people who got started building for their own enjoyment and to make the games they want to play are now old and skilled enough to join us as designers and developers, with unique skills in particular game-building tasks.

We can assemble Ocean's 11-type teams – find the best people at specific tasks and bring them together for the duration of that project.

I should add that the free accessibility of these tools means we're seeing fantastic talent worldwide, including in developing countries. This is not only good for the builder economy, but also for diversifying content for everyone.

ID: There are more and earlier opportunities for young people to start their own businesses – innovating ways of making money from games, or creating virtual clothes, from their own bedrooms. As American entrepreneur Gary Vaynerchuk says, "the great resignation is a short term trend. The great never-applying-in-the-first-place is the long term play that most businesses aren't understanding."

MW: This flywheel of more developers building more games and experiences, bringing more players into the platform, increasing the payout to developers – rinse and repeat – is resulting in an explosion of content, which is a two-edged sword. It makes discovery more and more difficult – just as it happened in YouTube and the app stores – but it also creates upward pressure for quality in order to stand out.

What changes or evolution have you seen in the UK children's media environment in the past 25 years – particularly the digital/interactive/games environment?

ID: For a variety of reasons, most of them global and not just in the UK, there are increasingly fewer opportunities to develop children's television series and fewer slots in TV schedules. The rise of YouTube channels, streaming services, FAST channels and such have made up for this to some extent, but it's also driven digital presence for an IP from being a nice-to-have to being a must-have.

In fact, because digital makes it cheaper to create and faster to get to market, a growing number of creative ideas are now online-first.

The audience has changed, as well. Video doesn't need to be 4k quality to succeed; kids are happy to watch TikToks shot on a smartphone. Games don't have to be AAA quality; they can look like 64-bit blocky Minecraft graphics (though Roblox is moving toward more realistic avatars). Kids love great narrative, they love deep engagement, they love the ability to be social in virtual spaces – and they understand that 'quality' has different meanings for different content or platforms.

100 Years Of BBC School Broadcasting

Dr Steven Barclay, Researcher, Local Trust, London

This year marks the centenary of the BBC's first school broadcast. School broadcasting was a major part of the education and media systems, but was never given the recognition it deserved by either. In fact, it was as significant an achievement in creative and intellectual terms as children's broadcasting.

School broadcasting provided radio and television series for use in UK schools as part of children's and adolescents' education. Almost all subjects were eventually covered, in a wide variety of genres, from drama to observational documentary to presenter-led studio presentations, animation and musical sequences. Only in the first few years however, did broadcasts resemble lessons or lectures.

The inter-war period, when school broadcasting was born, was a time of new ideas in education and our system of universal education was still being formed, as were ideas of pedagogy, child psychology and how education related to society. The 'progressive education' movement was primarily concerned with teaching practice, and its watchwords were experience, activity and individual expression. School broadcasting tried hard to fit in with this but, despite its popularity with the grassroots of teaching, was never quite accepted by education theorists.

BBC school broadcasting became immensely popular and by the 1960s was being used by very nearly all UK schools. The popularity of individual series, always aimed at a particular subject and age range, varied widely but some reached a very high proportion of their target audience; they were relied upon by teachers and influential in the curriculum.

This success was the product of a particular regulatory structure. The BBC was a publicly owned corporation with a royal charter. It was not part of government, but it did share with it a duty to provide a public service. School broadcasting was not required or requested by the charter or the government. The BBC assumed the responsibility itself and inadvertently became a public educational resource provider, in some ways a complement to the state school system that would become, in 1945, finally universal for both primary and secondary pupils up to the age of 15.

There was no clear idea of what to do at first – hence the broadcast lectures. The structure that developed was one in which BBC producers designed programmes, partly in collaboration with panels of teachers. The most significant early innovations however, Rhoda Power's dramatised history programmes and Ann Driver's *Music and Movement*, were driven by producers.

The fundamental question – how to turn media into education – was a difficult one. The BBC's answer was quite different to that of the later Children's Television Workshop – the BBC being more holistic and humanistic and less outcomes-based – though formally as inventive (the BBC, in *Look and Read* (1967) for example, used animation to teach initial literacy before *Sesame Street* did).

BBC school broadcasting benefited from being part of a large and powerful corporation with authority, resources and expertise, and was spurred on in 1957 when competitor ITV launched its own schools and colleges educational TV service.

There was much innovation, especially in the 1960s. *Look and Read* and *Words and Pictures* (1970–2007) pioneered phonics, later to become ubiquitous in classrooms. The geography series *People of Many Lands* (1959–1974) turned into a series of child-centred documentaries. Science series encouraged project work and active learning. English series promoted new writing. Ron Smedley's *Scene* used drama and documentary to engage pupils staying on at school to 16. *Tout Compris* (1973–77) had French teenagers voice fly-on-the-wall documentaries for language learning.

Briefly, educational broadcasting moved onto the government's agenda. For a period BBC2 (launched in 1967) was to be all or part educational, directly funded by the government. However, this did not transpire and the main thing that came out was the Open University, in which broadcasting played only a small part.

As the service expanded, some problems proved intractable. One was distribution. School series were aired in 20–30 minute programmes in morning and afternoon slots during school terms, which in the early days required schools to have a radio or television in the right classroom at the right time. Recording onto tape by schools transformed functionality but was expensive and governed by restrictive laws, not lifted till 1988.

Another problem was publications. Printed materials for teachers and learners accompanied almost all series. This made the BBC a large publisher – a role it did not have expertise or structure for. Producing and marketing publications was cumbersome and financially precarious; the BBC was committed to avoiding making a profit (while broadcasts were free to any school with a radio or television, publications were charged at cost price). The inflation of the 1970s wreaked havoc and the BBC struggled to make ends meet – leading to a series of co-production deals with educational publishers better suited to the task. This was a foretaste of the future.

During the 1980s the service reached a peak of popularity and effectiveness. Colour television, VCR and audio cassette recording and the gradual addition of series that worked well (some of which were very long running) had all added to utility. Uptake, already high from the 1960s, continued to increase marginally to near saturation point (almost 100% of schools used BBC school broadcasting, most taking multiple series). By this time over 140 different series were broadcast annually, over 900 broadcast hours. Sales of the most popular publications ran to the hundreds of thousands. The flexible topic-led series *Watch!* (1967–2009) was used by 73% of primary schools to structure their termly project, with the production team coordinating with libraries and local museums. *Words and Pictures* was being used by 88% of primary schools by 1989.

A turning point came at the end of the 1990s when the Education Act of 1988 and Broadcasting Act of 1990 marked new periods in both these arenas. The Education Act provided a national curriculum, the development of which had been controversial, and accompanied an increase of government control at the expense of teachers and resource providers. The BBC's greatest strengths: curriculum innovation, flexibility and alternative methods were no longer as valuable. The Broadcasting Act marked a change of direction that would lead to the end of educational imperative in the sector.

A transformative change emerged with digital media and the internet. In the 1990s the government invested heavily in educational technology in classrooms, providing interactive whiteboards, projectors and computers. School broadcasting's biggest barrier – distribution, was suddenly solved. Ironically it was at this point that the axe fell. It was a sign of the very different ethos that influenced the regulation of the internet compared to that which had influenced the birth of broadcasting.

Unlike schools themselves, where the principle of publicly funded provision was accepted, the educational resources used in schools had traditionally been provided by a commercial market. Because the BBC was an educational resource provider, technically it competed in this sector. While broadcasting was the preserve of the BBC, ITV and Channel 4 with their transmission privileges, this was less of a problem because there was little scope for competition. However, the internet was seen as a large new potential market by commercial providers. A consortium brought forward a legal challenge and this led eventually to the BBC in 2008 withdrawing an already well-developed *BBC Jam* project which had been aimed at moving its school broadcasting service online. Instead the BBC would now provide only study resources in the much reduced *Bitesize*. With this the tradition of long-form school broadcasting died out. *Bitesize* itself, however, was a relative success and remains widely used.

The real value of having a public service broadcaster was shown dramatically however, when the Covid-19 pandemic required all schools to close and children to undertake remote learning. The Department for Education asked the BBC to provide lockdown learning, which it did (though it did not resemble school broadcasting as it had been). Meanwhile the government also moved forward with its own service – taking over Oak National Academy and planning to use it as a form of nationalised resource provider. Ironically this is in turn now also facing a legal challenge from the commercial sector.

As with all children's content in the present time, anything that does not have a strong commercial appeal is facing great challenges. There is little sign of political appetite to increase public service media's funding and scope, nor of the government retreating from central control over schools and education.

School broadcasting was an extraordinary creative achievement – as well as being popular and cost effective. Its demise is a great loss. Two trends may point to a path back to a regulatory framework for media conducive to a similar flowering in the future. Firstly increasing school refusal indicates a growing realisation that an education system cannot be based exclusively on attendance at school. Secondly, cyberbullying, disinformation and the rise of destructive 'influencers' shows that regulation of digital online media for children has failed gravely. As long as the commercial streaming services and social media platforms have no reason to provide education as the broadcasters once did, children and our future are the losers.

Think writers should get paid for their hard work?

So do we.

That's why we've paid our members more than £700m since 1977.

Join today at alcs.co.uk

BBC Children's & Education:
Why Do We Care?

Patricia Hidalgo, Director of Children's & Education, BBC

Recently I was in a meeting with a senior politician to talk about our work and he asked me a really good question: why do you care? It was helpful because it made me pull back for a moment and reflect. Often our assumptions can become so baked into daily business that you start to forget them.

It isn't difficult for me to express why we care about our audience at BBC Children's & Education. Over the last few years we have made many changes, all with our audience in mind. Now seems a good moment to reflect on them, to see how they have stacked up.

We care so much about our audience that we have been prepared to radically redefine our children's TV business in order to keep reaching them with public service content. In headline terms this has meant our wholesale switch of attention away from linear channels and instead following the audience on-demand to focus on BBC iPlayer.

I'm delighted to say that we have had success. In the financial year 23/24, viewing of BBC Children's content has grown 24% on BBC iPlayer – and there's been a 17% increase in BBC iPlayer accounts accessing children's content. Overall, BBC Children's & Education content was streamed an amazing 2.2 billion times on iPlayer during 23/24.

I make no apology for what follows being an 'industry' piece, and for recapping things we have said in our commissioning briefings. We're the biggest commissioner of children's TV content in the UK, and I believe that everyone should know what we've been doing.

For public service content to matter, it has to be watched. It has to have an impact and it has to be relevant, which means getting the magic elixir of inform, educate and – especially – *entertain* exactly right. We absolutely want to boost children's intellects, but that alone won't take you very far. You have to be just as passionate about richly entertaining kids as educating them. Luckily, the UK is full of creative people who want to do just that.

To best reach kids in the on-demand world where they now live, we have properly moved over from running just a schedule to managing our library in iPlayer as well. If creating a schedule is like a game of draughts, managing a streaming library is more like 3D chess. It requires the right amount of titles, the right amount of genres, the right amount of box sets, the right amount of weekly episodes, and of course the right amount of new material. This last point is very important. With an 'everlasting' library, new programming has a different importance than it used to. It is completely different to the old linear equation of new = good and repeats = bad.

Being iPlayer-first gave us a different perspective on how much new content we needed across a year, along with when it should be released. It took us away from prior linear patterns where we would launch a raft of new series all at once for the start of a season.

We combined this new perspective with the most efficient use of our budget, in order to gauge the ideal mix of titles, episodes, ideas and production values that could cut through in a hypercompetitive market and make an impact on our audience. We were finally completing a journey that BBC Children's had been on for some years: fewer, bigger, better.

Simply put, brutal market realities mean there is no point making things if they won't land with the audience. Quality may be excellent, but if you create too many small things they will get lost. We needed to maintain this quality, but distil it into a tighter range of titles that could be sufficiently promoted and therefore discoverable.

Very importantly, this more focused range of titles and hours is still supported by the same commissioning budget. We are spending as much as we did three years ago, it's the emphasis that has changed. To help make the funding work and to capitalise on audience success we have committed to longer runs of series, with double-commissions for titles such as *Malory Towers*, *The Dumping Ground*, *Numberblocks* and *One Zoo Three*. We've done audience research more upfront to identify what is working and push on with commissions, rather than wait for series data to come in over a long period of time.

An essential component of enabling these changes has been the flexibility within Ofcom's new BBC Operating Licence. This has moved on from being a rigid framework of annual hours and sub-genres, and has been of great help in allowing us to focus resources and transition to be iPlayer-first. The growth that we've shown is, I hope, a testament to Ofcom's forward-thinking on this.

Over the past three years our commissioning focus has been on Drama, Animation and high-impact Factual. We have done this because they are the key components in making our *whole* public service offer attractive to children. I want to re-state this point about our whole offer. We commission now and will always commission a very wide range of content genres so that we bring the very best of everything to kids. But it is Drama, Animation and high-impact Factual that are the primary drivers in getting the audience to find and engage with our content.

Fortunately we were already tremendously strong in live action Drama for all ages, and for Animation with 0–6s. We lacked a UK public service offer in 7+ Animation and we've been seeking to address that in our commissioning and with the Ignite initiative. It's been a long road and we're seeing the green shoots of that coming through now.

Even in Drama we couldn't just sit back. Audience expectations have never been higher, thanks to the global streaming competition. We are always having to push hard to gain the production values and ambitious narratives we need. One way has been to raise the level of additional income to our slate. It has meant working with our indie suppliers across many different forms of international co-production, distributors, tax reliefs and financing support.

Together we have considerably increased the income that can be generated in this way, amounting to an additional 50% of value on top of our annual funding – double what we achieved last year and over three times what we have managed in the past. In so doing we have boosted the BBC's offer for children, against the headwinds of inflation. My thanks go to all who have put the extra effort into these time-consuming and often complex arrangements.

High-impact Factual is an area of great interest for us. We already have some highly successful brands in the form of *Operation Ouch*, *Horrible Histories* and Steve Backshall's *Deadly* series. We are always looking for more. Without doubt it's the hardest genre to punch through in, and we're delighted to have commissioned *Horrible Science* this year as an exciting new addition.

Another aspect to our changes has been how we commission, as well as what. In the past our commissioning team was closely involved in managing both the linear schedule and iPlayer library, putting pressure on their time as a result. Our new Content and Programming Strategy (CPS) team untethered them from this, allowing commissioning to focus on finding the very best projects. Now CPS manages the long term view, looking at what the iPlayer library needs and how commissioning can respond. We may, for instance, be over-served in one genre for the next couple years but then need to address a gap after that.

One great outcome for British children is the new agreement with Pact, whereby our titles live on iPlayer for four years before relicensing. This may seem like an operational detail but it helps us to build an attractive public service streaming library full of original British content, in the face of global giants who have the buying power to amass huge volumes of material. It's a good example of how the whole UK industry has worked together to get the best for the audience – and is something worth shouting about.

Acquisitions have an important role in building our library, and our intentions around these can often be misunderstood. Just as with getting the balance right between entertainment and 'pure' education, so too we need a balance of acquisitions and originals in our programming mix if we are to reach all UK children. We have actively set out to use acquisitions for three key purposes: great content that is attractive in and of itself; bringing kids titles from around the world that we could never make; giving us a boost in animation where our UK commissions have not yet come through. Some acquired titles are able to do all these three things at once.

We remain far and away the primary maker of UK original children's television content – compared to the whole of the rest of the children's sector, we are off the chart. And in the streaming world that we now inhabit, acquisitions are not substitutional. Once upon a time playing an acquired show on linear meant denying a slot for an originated show. But now there is room for everything. It's as-well-as not instead-of. Plus everyone will recall how acquisitions have long been a keystone of the BBC Children's offer, whether you grew up with *Scooby Doo* or *Rugrats*.

Returning to the iPlayer library, and all the various elements described above, we had to devise intertwined strategies for making all this content work in harmony – and for letting the audience know about it. We have titles such as *A Kind of Spark* and *Phoenix Rise* which drop all at once, while others are best served with episodic or batch drops like *Bluey* and *The Dumping Ground*. Some new series will spark an interest in older episodes, and on the flipside care is needed around titles migrating away from iPlayer. There is more to manage than ever!

We owe thanks to the BBC Marketing team as well, who have also evolved new approaches to meet our audience challenge. Children are scattered across a huge variety of platforms, and there is no choice but to use at least some of these if we are to reach them. In the absence of big tech-style budgets our Marketing team has been highly adept in using video messages in places like YouTube and gaming platforms, plus interactive mini-games, cinema moments and bigger BBC family campaigns, such as last year's *Screens – It's What's On Them That Counts*.

Even with this marketing activity, the multitude of digital spaces requires us to find other ways of being where the audience is. We created a Digital Media Platforms & Planning team. Their role is to raise the awareness of our key content titles, using different means depending on the platform type. Their work ranges from *Operation Ouch* website games, showing how the gut works, teen-friendly TikToks, featuring the cast of *The Next Step*, and a new BBC Roblox experience.

Planning this support is key, or there is the risk of diluting activities across the endless sea of digital platforms. It goes back to the heart of fewer, bigger, better and being focused on only supporting the right number of titles. There is something about making the right amount of content in the first place that drives everything else, and prevents effort from being spread too thinly.

While the children's media world is highly digital we do seek to reach kids in real-life too. Wherever possible we are working with partners to create off-screen experiences that can provide long-lasting family memories. We have built out from the CBeebies Prom at the Royal Albert Hall. It played at 11 UK venues in 2023 and will reach a further 20 this year. Even CBBC has had a Prom now, with the *Horrible Histories* team performing *'Orrible Opera* last July, and now a special *Quentin Blake's Box of Treasures* orchestral performance taking place at the Barbican this summer.

Operation Ouch has had its own long-running exhibition at the Manchester Museum of Science and Industry with the digestion-themed *Food, Poo and You*. It too will be travelling to other locations. And even reading has hit the road with our *CBeebies Bedtime Stories* tent becoming a feature of family-friendly festivals such as Gloworm, Bestival and even Glastonbury.

I said that I would come back with further reflections on why we care about public service content. For me it is a combination of serving both the audience and UK culture, and so helping to protect both. Historically the UK has enjoyed a strong domestic TV industry, in which funding and culture have been aligned. But what happens when the money moves elsewhere? That's what we're seeing now in children's media both here and abroad, particularly as the global streamers have retreated from kids commissioning. Who safeguards the culture when the money has moved on?

Public service broadcasting is a big part of the answer, and I have observed internationally that PSBs have grown in importance again as catalysts to get projects moving. They are the organisations who actually care about children and culture, in the face of global market withdrawal. It will be interesting to see how this plays out in the next few years.

For now, our British project goes on. Today, in the interests of space, I have deliberately focused only narrating the changes made to our children's TV offer. I could do the same article all over again for BBC Education. It too has had changes and successes: *Bitesize* on target, *500 Words* at Buckingham Palace, the new version of *micro:bit*. Most exciting of all are the changes we are planning to *BBC Bitesize* as it passes the quarter-century mark – so I am already looking forward to writing the second part of this article!

Why Edutainment Matters

Ahrani Logan, CEO, Peapodicity and
Sam Harris, Director, Auger Insights

We need to start thinking differently about 'edutainment' in 2024. It isn't a dirty word.

The *Oxford English Dictionary* classifies 'edutainment' as

> "products such as books, television programs and especially computer software that both educate and entertain."

For some, the thought of edutainment brings to mind clunky, boring and try-hard content experiences.

To be fair, it is quite an old concept: Walt Disney used the term 'edutainment' back in 1954 to describe his multi-Academy-award-winning nature documentary series, *True Life Adventures*. Edutainment via TV and film has been around for a long time. Shows such as *Sesame Street*, *Dora the Explorer* and *Teletubbies* have helped teach kids for generations.

However, it feels like education is becoming more and more important with each passing year. Why? It's a good question, with a surprisingly simple answer: the world is changing.

Today's media content providers have a whole new audience to cater to. Generation Z is growing up. Generation Alpha has arrived. And these groups are engaging with a range of new challenges – challenges that edutainment may be well placed to address.

In 2024 kids' lives are complex

At Auger Insights, we regularly run focus groups, trend workshops and media watch-alongs with young people around the world – and the complexity of their lives is always astonishing.

A glance through the news reveals just some of the issues young people today face: the Education Policy Institute reported in their *Annual Review 2023* that primary aged learners' outcomes in maths remained well below pre-pandemic norms. Social pressures have resulted in an increased focus on identity, reality and mental health. The quantity of information, and access to it, has vastly increased – and with it a flow of troubling misinformation and disinformation. Misogyny is on the rise among boys. Body anxiety is growing in girls. AI tools are evolving, complex and potentially scary.

Edutainment can help young people tackle topics like these head on – providing spaces that are safe and engaging. It can assist them in processing the modern world and their place within it. And, when done well, it can do all this in a way that blends perfectly into kids' modern lives and needs.

Edutainment can get into the spaces that matter

Young people are spending an increasing amount of time on screens – watching TV and films, playing games, scrolling on social media. The best edutainment content can surreptitiously sit within these spaces, offering constructive experiences that can be as enlightening as they are exciting.

Examples of such content include BookTok, which appears to be leading the current charge towards increasing reader engagement. 'BookTokers' now form a sub-community on social media platform TikTok. They focus on books and literature, making short and often visually captivating and entertaining videos. According to research by the Publishers Association in October 2022, almost two-thirds (59%) of 16–25 year olds say that these 'bookfluencers' have helped them discover a passion for reading and new titles, with over half turning to BookTok (55%) for recommendations. Bookstores are even designating bookshelf space to the 'TikTok Chart'. Edutainment is making commercial sense.

Another reason that edutainment matters is that it can cater to different learning styles and across different age groups by leveraging the power of play.

Language learning platform and app, Duolingo, is appealing to older kids (and adults) through quick and easy to use lessons. Duolingo ABC, for the youngest audiences, has gamified the process of learning to read. PBS Kids offers the largest library of educational games for kids aged two to eight – their approach is based on the belief that games can reinforce the lessons that kids are learning in a TV show. Similarly, digital products by Lego, Roblox and Minecraft, encourage creativity, motor skills, and spatial recognition.

Meeting the audience at their interest level is key. What are children passionate about? Gamified learning appears to be natural and intuitive to these young digital natives. If you have ever witnessed a toddler tapping and swiping a handheld device, you might recognise this as an evolution of the human experience, in real time.

Evolving edutainment – from XR to AI and beyond

New technology is enabling us to push the boundaries of edutainment even further.

XR (eXtended Reality), AR (Augmented Reality) and VR (Virtual Reality) technologies are continually improving, fostering curiosity in young minds. They work by using wonder – tapping into young people's emotional response – to create memorable learning experiences.

The rise of AI has touched so many areas and edutainment has not escaped. Potential benefits include the creation of personalised learning experiences, catering to individual children. This can create unique and powerful ways to engage with content – for instance, PBS Kids is exploring how to integrate AI into digital episodes of *Lyla in the Loop* to create richer learning opportunities for its audiences.

However, the ethical implications of this new technology is vast. There is potential to misuse AI by communicating inaccurate information or promoting biased content. Discrimination against certain groups can occur when AI algorithms go unchecked.

Ongoing conversations about new technologies and their roles in society illustrate how positive learning outcomes can only be achieved where accountability and transparency are first and foremost. And this is particularly important when it comes to youth media.

Powering up traditional education structures

Schools too have recognised the value of edutainment. Many have switched from traditional learning to more visual, engaging, hands-on and multimodal methods.

Benefits in the classroom include easy introductions to trickier concepts, especially in the science, technology, engineering and maths, or STEM, subject areas. Increased engagement and the motivation to learn makes well-made edutainment an easy choice in the school environment. Who wouldn't want to make learning fun?!

Anecdotal evidence collected by *AugmentifyIt* AR, the multi-award-winning augmented reality brand with a 'Play to Learn' ethos, has yielded some important finds. Children are still talking about science lessons in the playground, following the use of *AugmentifyIt* AR cards. Imagine TV edutainment being talked about in this way. Creating, connecting and collaborating with companies who have entered and succeeded in the school space can help extend IP and brands. According to the Association of Child Psychotherapists, school is the single most important place in the lives of most children aside from home. Edutainment can act as a bridge between the learning and entertainment worlds. Children's media probably needs to recognise this and utilise it more.

Building empathy and unlocking new perspectives

Finally, one of the more important things that edutainment can help with is the understanding of difference – enabling young people to explore various opinions, situating themselves within the wider world and empowering a belief in their own abilities and identities.

It can help children explore a range of cultures and perspectives, building empathy for those living in different countries and situations. It also affords the opportunity to debate and differentiate between opinions that *appear* intolerant and opinions that are intolerant. Edutainment can offer a powerful tool, shedding light on the world, offering guidance and helping to make young people's navigations through life a little less scary.

And while edutainment has a strong role in unlocking different perspectives, content that reflects the reality and references of kids' own lives is also hugely important. Edutainment can help young people see themselves – in terms of culture, identity and background – in the world around them. Building the crucial 'see it to be it' role models that infuse the confidence and energy needed by young minds to achieve their dreams and ambitions, and to tackle a changing, accelerating world.

Photo by stem.T4L on Unsplash

How do we start 'thinking differently' about edutainment?

So how do we best create educational content that engages young people? That leverages the platforms, characters and concepts that they love, to help them better connect with and understand the world around them? How do we create entertaining, informative media that is just as enjoyable as a game of *Battle Royale* on Fortnite or a new Roblox 'obby'?!

How do we use the edutainment wins from other youth content genres and create vivid, fun, engaging and memorable viewer experiences?

The rise of technology signals the ushering in of a new 'Golden Age of Edutainment', empowering children to become socially confident, lifelong learners, who use their critical thinking skills and empathy to help create a better world. We are almost a quarter of the way into the 21st Century. Now is the time that we, the media industry, should become the ushers.

The recent and much publicised return of *Dora the Explorer* is just the beginning. It's time to accelerate. It's time to start 'thinking differently'.

A special thank you to Cerys Griffiths (BBC Education), Professor Dr Ger Graus OBE and Dr Kevin Clark, for contributing to this article and sharing their expertise on why edutainment matters in 2024.

Legacy Of YACF: Two And A Half Years Later

Jackie Edwards, Children's Media Specialist, Former Head of YACF, BFI

It's been two and half years since the *Young Audiences Content Fund* (YACF) was suddenly killed off by Nadine Dorries, and two and a half years since the CMF's first slew of queries along the lines of 'WTF?' to both Houses of Parliament was met with the reassurance that the efficacy of the Fund would be assessed 'swiftly and thoroughly' by the government.

Bigger Picture Research's independent evaluation that ran alongside the Fund Pilot declared it a success, that it provided proof of concept that highly targeted funding, administered with rigour within a clear framework of strategic priorities, is capable of delivering social and economic value as intended, but the government has been terribly quiet on their assessment of that assessment, or any sort of assessment since then. (Two and a half years ago, did I say?)

A funny thing happened at the Voice of the Listener and Viewer (VLV) Spring Conference the other day. Dame Caroline Dineage gave a speech. You know, ex-Minister of State at the Department for Culture, Media & Sport (DCMS), currently Chair of the cross-party DCMS Select Committee Caroline Dineage? Daughter of Fred Dineage off of *How* (1966–81; 1990–2006; 2020–22). Yes, her. She was discussing the state of children's public service media (PSM) and described how there had been a lovely reboot of *How*, produced for ITV, two series in fact – her dad was in it! – but then the money suddenly wasn't there and no more series of *How* were produced, and it was sad. Dame Caroline was talking about the two series of *How* that had been funded in large part by the Young Audiences Content Fund. Subsequent series weren't funded because… well… ask Nadine. I put my hand up to try and explain, but sadly wasn't called upon. I hope someone is able to join the dots between funding and a show being made or not made for Dame Caroline. Maybe someone at the DCMS could help?

Sorry for the terrible digression from the original intention of this piece, but it is a story that not only grimly entertains, but also informs and educates us on the lack of joined up thinking, or indeed care, on the whole subject of PSM for young audiences and how it gets made in this country.

Aside from that eyebrow raising story, there was a lot to enjoy at the VLV. Best of all was to see *Mixmups* (2023) pick up the award for Best Children's Programme. *Mixmups* is a glorious and joyful stop frame animated show for Milkshake!, delivered by the animation gods at Mackinnon & Saunders.

CHILDREN'S MEDIA YEARBOOK **2024**

*Stills from **Mixmups***

Mixmups creator Rebecca Atkinson wanted to make a show that was a truthful and authentic representation of disability, knowing how important it is for all children to see themselves on screen – it makes them feel seen, it makes them feel valued. Even though there are an estimated 150 million children worldwide with a disability, shows like this don't get made – a bit 'niche' for those that put commerce before childhood.

Rebecca's kind words in her acceptance speech described *Mixmups* as a testament to what the YACF could do. It's the sort of show that needs to be made. Representation works, it reflects, it reassures, it normalises everyone's life experience. I am so pleased that series one was made but, like Dame Caroline, I am sad that a second series is not currently happening, though unlike Dame Caroline, I do know why. Without support or intervention from something like a YACF, few shows will be made in the UK, and no animated shows like *Mixmups*, that do something different and good. As for domestically focussed, live action shows – the lovely factual and entertainment shows that exquisitely and specifically reflect and celebrate UK audiences… good luck with that.

© Mackinnon and Saunders

That is the bleak reality of where we are just now.

But chins up, lads, we must be hopeful. Regional funding is continuing to support development and some production. Indeed, most recent on the scene is the *Creative Wales Young Content Fund*, launched in 2022 following the demise of the YACF. Its purpose is to offer funding and support to Welsh independent production companies to develop bilingual 'full length' content in Welsh and English – both live action and animation – for young audiences. Da iawn!

Undoubtedly the sector needs more.

CMF's recent summit on the future of PSM for young audiences discussed the double jeopardy we face – how do we fund content and then where should we put it so kids can find it? We'll leave the finding for another day, but the funding seems to me to be reasonably straightforward.

At the summit a number of levers that could be pulled to stimulate commissions and/or fund shows were discussed. A popular lever was enhanced tax credits (great, but only great if you have a commission or can self-commission – BBC/BBC Studios I'm looking at you – it's only a part of the funding, and is not currently specific to PSM content), less popular was the re-introduction of quotas on the grounds that people won't like it, could create a fiscal drag on commercial public service broadcasters (PSBs) (I say tough, you want to wear a PSB badge and the prominence that goes with it, you have to pay for it, and children's content should be a critical part of your output – it's a societal thing, like a… public service), but most sensible was a modified YACF, a 2.0 if you will. If you want specific, targeted funding that can stimulate commissions, or fully support production maybe, funding that can be accessible to production companies from around the UK, celebrating regional communities and indigenous languages, supporting shows of all genres and techniques and sizes and shapes, it's the way to do it. It's not hard to move the dials, adapt support for the changing landscape – it's a direct and specific intervention that does what needs to be done.

But "what will it cost?" I hear you ask. It depends on how much ambition we have as an industry, and how much the next government wants to do something to enrich the lives of a generation that has endured such neglect in so many ways over the last 14 years.

We should talk less about funding and start really talking about value. Every £1 of TV tax credit returns £8.50 back to the economy. The YACF delivers similar in its most modest estimation, in its most realistic calculation it returns around £11 per £1 invested. (BTW, this estimate excludes broadcast re-licensing, impact from development activity, licensing & merchandising, tourism…)

So… if it creates jobs, provides training, stimulates the economy *and* enriches the lives of our young – can we afford not to do it?

The State Of Children's TV In The UK

 **Di Redmond**, Writer and Non-Executive Director, ALCS

The decline of children's and young people's TV is a loss that will be felt by children throughout the country, as well as the nation as a whole. The closure of popular children's channel CITV, the removal of CBBC from terrestrial TV and the rapid take up of streaming services such as Netflix, Disney+, Max and Paramount with YouTube leading the way, marked the end of an era that began in the early post-war years when entertaining and educating children was seen by the Government as a priority.

BBC children's introduced iconic TV favourites – *Andy Pandy, Bill and Ben, Play School, Magic Roundabout, Captain Pugwash, Postman Pat, Byker Grove,* among many others. Regional television Granada, YTV, Anglia, Central and S4C also became a reliable source of funding for many new groundbreaking live action and animated shows. An entire industry thrived, providing work for both in-house and freelance writers, animators, actors, voiceover artists, puppeteers and illustrators.

As the industry gathered momentum, Britain was exporting programmes worldwide and our status on the back of *Balamory, Fireman Sam, Bob the Builder, Postman Pat, Peppa Pig, Thomas the Tank Engine, Teletubbies* and so many more groundbreaking shows was second to none. Our programme output and subsequent sales (especially in merchandise goods for the under-fives) brought in huge international tie-ins and co-production deals. Iconic producers and commissioners, such as Anne Wood, Cynthia Felgate, Theresa Plummer-Andrews and Anna Home, supported the creation of acclaimed series that were aired worldwide.

The closure of children's TV channels and the recent shuttering of the BFI Young Audience Content Fund has changed the landscape. Previously, the established process for pitching primetime TV content was to develop a show with engaging characters, the best storytelling, plus a celeb to front it, picture books that coincided with transmission, plus a tonne of merchandising. Such commissions for a 13, 26, or even 54 episode series are a thing of the past. Viewing habits, particularly among young people, have changed considerably.

So as the death knell for children's TV plays out, the tragedy is that we still need this treasured art form more than ever before. So many organisations, investors, politicians, writers, artists and the public itself are voicing their sense of loss, disappointment and indignation. Public service broadcasters (PSB) have a duty to produce quality content for children. In the case of the BBC, we pay money through our licence fee for the promotion of children's TV. Where has that money gone? We're still paying our licence fee to the government but there's very little kids' TV to show for it.

It was reassuring to hear Labour MP Thangham Debbonaire speak in parliament on the demise of children's public service content, flagging the dramatic changes in viewing habits, particularly in the area of over-sevens, where parents no longer control viewing as they do with under-fives. Good content "provides powerful information on role models, inspires ambition, encourages social inclusion, and develops a child's understanding of self and community". Debonnaire regretted the long term reduction in commissions for original UK content for children's TV, that traditionally made a big contribution to our economy.

Debbonaire's not wrong! We can still remember when TV sales were global and our reputation as quality broadcasters was second to none. Pouring millions into the economy, children's TV was respected and applauded. Jackie Cockle, who produced *Bob the Builder*, received a BAFTA for her long-running stop-frame animated series generated out of Manchester and Altrincham. This was a time when children weren't sidelined; quite the opposite, they were big time. It was a golden age when kids had a voice that resonated.

Writing for under-fives is rich and vast, and the merchandise pay-off for broadcasters seeking tie-ins and co-productions is lucrative. *Postman Pat* socks and slippers, *Thomas the Tank Engine* biscuits, Bob's safety helmet, Peppa Pig's toothbrush, the list is endless. The industry in effect fed itself. As a result of our national reputation for good content, British broadcasters and their successes were on the global stage: MIPCOM, Cartoon Forum, Kidscreen and the European Broadcasting Union. Serious money was invested in films and television series across all the channels and our reputation as creatives boomed.

So why did the star fall from the sky? The decline can be attributed to a lack of development funding and interest in commissioning, the increasing dominance of streaming and video sharing platforms and the subsequent change in viewing habits, particularly for young people. Technological and societal changes have profoundly changed the way that children and young people view content. TV viewing among 4–15 year olds has fallen by 62% in the last five years alone, as they increasingly use video sharing platforms and subscription streaming services to access their content.

This has undoubtedly been used as a justification to cut public service broadcaster's children's TV budgets. But a lack of funding for quality programmes will only accelerate this trend, as young people are presented with fewer alternatives to streaming, with damaging consequences.

According to Ofcom figures, first-run UK originated children's programming on PSB channels like BBC and ITV fell to an all time low in 2022, down to 518 hours compared to 640 in 2019. Spending on original UK children's content has also fallen from £114 million in 2013 to £80 million in 2022.

In total the Young Audience Content Fund provided £44m in funding to the children's media sector. The fund, which was intended to help UK children's TV compete on the global stage, covered up to 50% of the production costs. Its closure has had a highly damaging effect on the sector, and combined with the UK's exclusion from the EU's Creative Europe scheme as a result of Brexit, means that development funding is no longer available on the levels it once was.

Instead of increased funding to support grassroots children's TV content from the ground up, the government has instead opted for a system of tax credits to stimulate production. This is welcome but insufficient, particularly as tax credits will disproportionately benefit existing productions, often from overseas.

As my colleague on the Board of ALCS, Helen Blakeman, says:

> "Whilst increased tax credits are a major boon for the children's and creative sector, they're not the sole solution. Until the industry works together to establish a multi-purpose plan, with the input and support from the multi-layered big-hitters of government, 'broadcast' media, subscription video on demand services and digital platforms then the sector, the audience, and the writers will continue to suffer."

Lack of funding is obvious, but worse than that is lack of interest – lack of care. Kids always get the worst deal. Whatever the genre, if anything has to go then it's children first – hey, they're little, they won't notice and eventually they won't even remember. Our children are so precious, so vulnerable and so brilliant. We owe them more than lip service; it is our duty and the government's responsibility to give them quality programmes – that is their right.

This sentiment is also echoed by Helen Blakeman:

> "Children's TV in the UK, however, is a bit like the NHS; it's a national treasure and it helps to shape our society. Without it, we wouldn't be the nation that we are. But times and viewing habits change. The golden age is behind us, and now it's up to the industry and the broadcasters to help shape the future of children's viewing. It's also vital that British children are able to see their lives reflected back on-screen in all its glorious diversity, and, crucially, that it's free to access."

The government must engage with the children's TV sector and plan a credible path forward for this essential but endangered part of our cultural sector and national heritage. The restoration of desperately needed development funding would be an excellent starting point.

Failure isn't an option. We owe it to our children to ensure that they have access to quality content that reflects their lived experiences. What does it say about our society if we are no longer able to provide this? As Vicky Ireland, Ambassador and Trustee for *Action for Children's Arts* says:

> "Children are citizens with rights. We have signed up to the 54 Articles of the UN Convention on the Rights of the Child, including Article 31 that states: 'Every child has the right to relax, play and take part in a wide range of cultural and artistic activities'. This includes their right and need to have their own media sector and access to quality public service content. We must find a way to make this happen. If we neglect and ignore the imagination and needs of our young, we restrict all our futures."

> **"We owe our children more than lip service; it is our duty and the government's responsibility to give them quality programmes – that is their right."**

Young Voices And Content Classification: The Future Of Age Ratings

Dr Chris Davies, Compliance Manager, BBFC and
Dr Wallis Seaton, Senior Compliance and Education Officer, BBFC

The British Board of Film Classification's age ratings have been part of the film-viewing experience in the UK for over 112 years. Many of us will think of being at the cinema, popcorn or ice cream in hand as trailers tease upcoming attractions and then, as the lights go down and voices hush, the BBFC Black Card appears, displaying the film's title and age rating and heralding that the magic is about to begin. Others may remember childhood trips to the video store and looking up at the covers of 18-rated videos that we were too young to rent. Or for audiences today, they may picture the BBFC symbol and content advice flickering onto the screen as they start the latest binge-watch on Netflix.

As times change, so do audiences and their tastes. Behaviour that used to be commonplace in films and TV is no longer seen as acceptable today, while content once deemed suitable only for adults may now appear tame by teens raised on more modern examples. Although these changes are often incremental, they can feel significant to those whose priority is the wellbeing of young people.

Our core mission at the BBFC is to help audiences choose what's right for them. We primarily do this by providing age ratings for films, series and other content released in cinemas; on physical media (DVDs, Blu-ray); or online, including on Netflix, Amazon Prime Video and AppleTV+. We also create content advice for every film and series we classify, including a detailed breakdown of the issues they contain, available on our website and app. Together, these resources empower people to make informed viewing decisions and help protect vulnerable audiences from potentially harmful content.

Researching what UK audiences want and expect from age ratings

For our age ratings to be useful they must accurately reflect society's evolving attitudes. Every four to five years, therefore, we reach out to thousands of people across the UK to learn what audiences want and expect at each of our age rating categories. We then amend our standards, embodied in our published Classification Guidelines, to ensure we best reflect the views of people today.

In March this year we published the results of our biggest guidelines review to date. Through our research partner, We are Family, we spoke to 12,000 people across the UK via a range of methodologies, including focus groups, cinema screenings and an online community.

Integral to this research, and all our work, is hearing and understanding the views of young people. Alongside focus groups with young people, we held viewing parties with 13–19 year olds in which a lead teen was recruited by our researchers to moderate and host a film party at home with a group of their friends. Depending on their age range, each was assigned an age-appropriate film to watch with their friends before recording the group answering a series of questions via an app on their phone. This created a fun and relaxed atmosphere for them to share their thoughts on the films and relevant content issues away from the typical focus group environment.

11,434 people, including 16–19 year olds, participated in an online survey that included questions exploring viewing habits, issues of concern and content-specific questions relating to a clip or trailer embedded in the survey. 97% of respondents said they saw value in content being age rated, with 99% recognising at least one of our age rating symbols and 78% recognising them all. With this recognition also comes trust: 85% of respondents said they trust BBFC age ratings when making viewing decisions all or most of the time, with that number rising to 88% among 16–19 year olds. Among parents this reached 90%, a 7% increase from our 2019 guidelines consultation. Similarly, 83% of people surveyed said they agreed with BBFC ratings all or most of the time, with those numbers even higher among older teens (85%), parents (87%) and teachers (87%).

Our research also provides insight into the issues of most concern to UK audiences, and in 2024 sexual violence remains at the top of the list. Suicide and self-harm, however, has risen from the 2019 results to become the second biggest area of concern – especially among young people – and there is widespread support for how the BBFC is classifying content with these challenging subjects. Teachers, parents and young people saw value in how content such as *Ackley Bridge* and *Words on Bathroom Walls* broached material relating to consent, abusive behaviour, mental health and suicide in a sensitive and empathetic manner. Participants felt young viewers could learn from and relate to such content, making them useful catalysts to complex conversations.

Violence and sex were also ranked highly in the list. People regularly erred on the side of caution for borderline scenes of violence, preferring a higher rating for content they deemed intense, impactful, tonally dark or notably bloody, sadistic or distressing. Teens who viewed *The Woman King*, for instance, agreed with the BBFC's 15 rating and did not want to see such content rated 12A. Similarly, on the 12A/15 borderline, people were concerned by scenes of sex. We have therefore updated our guidelines to reflect a slightly more cautious approach to classifying sex scenes if they are of longer duration, contain sexual detail or nudity, or if the sex appears rough or aggressive.

At PG, language was also felt to be an issue. The concern among participants, especially parents, was that certain terms could be normalised among young children who may then repeat them and cause offence. We are therefore adopting a stricter position, with certain words previously classified at PG now requiring a 12A.

While these changes are relatively minimal, they represent subtle shifts in societal attitudes and will ensure that our classification decisions continue to reflect the expectations of UK audiences.

Helping young people learn – and learning from them too

Our ongoing work is not limited to classifying content, however, and nor is our engagement with young people restricted to research projects. Our Education and Outreach programmes seek to educate and inform young people through activities and resources at home, in schools and as part of film festivals. This is mutually beneficial, as we are constantly learning and gathering more information from the people we engage with to understand their concerns and understand how best to provide them with the information and support they need to navigate a media-saturated world safely.

The BBFC Youth Panel is a cornerstone of this approach. Composed of 20 film enthusiasts aged 15–21, the group works closely with us to articulate the views of younger audiences and what matters to them. We meet with our panellists several times a year, in person and online, exploring key classification issues, our research and other elements of our work. In return, we present them with opportunities to see and discuss films with us; create podcasts; go behind the scenes of the classification process; meet industry professionals; and contribute to important forums, such as the BBFC's Advisory Panel on Children's Viewing – a group of leading experts in child welfare and development.

We also seek to harness the views, passion and creativity of young people. Our 'Create The Card' competition involves a nationwide search for young people to design their own BBFC Black Card for an upcoming film release. In 2023, for instance, over 700 children aged 4–11 submitted designs to accompany *Puss In Boots: The Last Wish*, with the winning entry announced by the film's star, Antonio Banderas, and appearing before all UK cinema screenings of the film.

Our website is home to a wealth of useful classification topic guides, case studies and podcasts, as well as classroom-ready resources

Toby K's winning Black Card entry

including PSHE-accredited lesson plans for Key Stage 1 through to Key Stage 4. We also provide online seminars tailored to primary, secondary or further education audiences, as well as in-person presentations, including introducing films at festivals, such as those hosted by Into Film. These interactive sessions provide a valuable introduction to film and video regulation in the UK, as well as what classification means in practice and why it is important. In doing so, we pull back the curtain of what the BBFC does and encourage young people to think differently about the content they watch.

Looking to the future

Our standards are truly shaped by the audience, and maintaining and even increasing such high levels of trust has been a key achievement for us over a turbulent few years for the entertainment industry. Just as UK audiences and the way we consume content changes over time, so too does the BBFC. We continue to expand into the online space, explore new technologies to support the classification process, and engage with audiences to ensure our age ratings remain valued and serve their purpose in protecting vulnerable viewers from harm. We want you to feel confident when making viewing decisions and enjoy what you watch, and hope that the children benefiting from today's age ratings will grow up to hold them in the same regard as adults. So whether you're heading to the cinema or settling in for a family movie night at home, the BBFC is here to help.

We're proud to support the Children's Media Foundation and the incredible work they do.

Children's media plays an important role in preparing our kids for their futures. With a media landscape that's changing fast, their work has never been more necessary.

OUR SERVICES

Research & Strategy

Creative

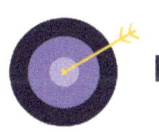
Marketing

We are Family is the world's biggest full-service agency group specialising in kids, teens, and families.

HelloUK@we-are-family.com
www.we-are-family.com

The UK's Local Television Network: A Hidden Gem In The Public Broadcasting Landscape For Young Audiences?

Jill Hurst, Creator and Series Producer of *Generation Genome*, KMTV and Doctoral Researcher, University of Kent

Nestled among the broadcasting giants with prime electronic programming guide (EPG) positions of 7 and 8, the Local Television Network (LTVN) has gone quietly about its business for more than a decade. With 34 Ofcom licensed stations in all four nations, the LTVN delivers a free to access service with a household reach of 16.2 million. Without public funding and huge cultural shifts in television viewing habits, it is nothing short of remarkable that this hardy collective has managed to survive.

This fight for survival is all too familiar to those of us working in the children's television sector. Policy and practice have thus far failed to offer lasting solutions. The BFI Young Audiences Content Fund (YACF) – introduced to redress the gap in public service content for children and young people – was a promising new horizon before its abrupt closure.[1] The YACF supported the creation of 61 brand new commissions, the development of 160 more and provided a vital lifeline to independent production companies. This included KMTV, one of the smaller LTVN stations. Like many, we mourned the loss of the scheme, for ourselves and for our viewers. Yet the strong connection the YACF stimulated between KMTV and children's media remains a continuing legacy. So much so that myself and others find ourselves increasingly asking whether local television could be a hidden gem on the public broadcasting landscape for young audiences.

Before the YACF existed, I was working as a research impact professional at the University of Kent, tasked with finding ways to support the institution's strategic objectives for civic engagement through KMTV. A university owned community television station transmitting across Kent and Medway, threading research into its flagship news and current affairs programmes was straightforward. As public funding subsidies fell away however, the channel rapidly needed to find alternative ways to generate income and remain sustainable. Civic engagement was no longer enough.

I was interested in developing journalistically led documentaries with KMTV, where short form pieces could translate academic outputs into engaging television content, including for young

---

[1] Young Audiences Content Fund Pilot (2022). *End Of Term Evaluation. Bigger Picture Research*.

audiences. This established a new creative portfolio and production skills that enabled KMTV to access the YACF and enter the children's television market.

The YACF sought to address key deficiencies identified by Ofcom's Children's content review (2018), including a lack of original, high-quality programmes for older children that would help them to understand the world by seeing themselves and their own lives reflected on their screens. It advocated for audiences and inclusivity both in terms of reach and significance and it focussed on the development of skills, training, employability and career pathways for early stage creatives. These goals, for many of us at LTVN, remain key to the future of children's content. The parallels between the overall values, vision and practice of KMTV (and LTVN) and those in the YACF brief were unmistakable. Once we had a concept, writing the bid was uncomplicated.

We developed *Generation Genome*, a six-episode journalistically led factual series made in collaboration with world-leading scientists and co-produced with more than 1000 students from schools across the UK. Our audience was woven into the production through hyperlocal narratives that were scouted and scripted by a small team of broadcast journalists and filmmakers. Equipment and crew were kept light and tight so the team could respond and adapt to stories and locations quickly and sustainably.

Like the YACF, a key goal for the LTVN is to create content that reaches, reflects, connects and engages diverse audiences and communities.

We designed case study packages that offered a platform for inclusion of young people from low socioeconomic households and underrepresented groups, including ethnically diverse youngsters, those with disabilities, young carers and/or those identifying as LGBTQIA+. A follow-up series, *Generation Why*, saw two members of our young audience, both aged 14, take on presenting roles. The first, Sadgun Sri Chandrapatla, was born in India but staying in Bradford. Our second presenter, Alex Black came from a deprived neighbourhood in Manchester.

The LTVN was already a career platform with a proven record of acting as a springboard for newly qualified graduate journalists to access major broadcasters globally. *Generation Genome* replicated this model more broadly for the creative industries, culminating in a year-long television training programme. KMTV is now a place where entry-level professionals can develop practical production skills, taking on roles they would not ordinarily have until much later in their careers.

Not all children and young people are served well by large public service broadcasting television services, particularly those in hard-to-reach areas and populations. The LTVN can play a vital role in keeping people and communities connected through trusted television content. More than half of the network's audience fall within socioeconomic bands C2 to E. This is important for the distribution of children's media since we know that poverty at any stage leads to negative outcomes and detrimentally impacts quality of life.[2] For young audiences, there is an evidential gap in educational

---

[2] Joseph Rowntree (2023). UK Poverty 2023. https://www.jrf.org.uk/uk-poverty-2023-the-essential-guide-to-understanding-poverty-in-the-uk

Generation Why: crew and panel with presenter Sadgun Sri Chandrapatla, aged 14 (panel centre)

attainment by parental income across all stages of learning. The pandemic widened this gap. The most disadvantaged young people in the UK are worse off than ever before.

A significant driver of this inequity is the digital divide. In the UK, an estimated 3.9 million children live in poverty. Increasingly, households will forgo broadband to prioritise spending elsewhere. Free-to-access local television might be the only time young people ever truly see themselves and their communities together with the issues they care about reflected on screen.

With the removal of the YACF, public service media commissions for young audiences decreased to pre-fund levels. Two fundamental challenges for children's content remain: who will fund it and where will we put it?

When we talk about making and distributing quality British content for children, very rarely is the LTVN mentioned. With its dual offer of linear and digital, and soon to be UK wide reach as a free-to-access, Ofcom regulated, public service platform, it becomes easier to appreciate how the LTVN might offer a new way to support children's television.

Perhaps now is the time for the children's media sector and the LTVN to come together with policy makers to ask: could the Local Television Network be a hidden gem on the public broadcasting landscape for young audiences?

This is Creative.
This is Wales.

We are working hard to make Wales the best place for creativity to thrive.

Our screen and animation industry is booming but there's plenty of room for more!

With our stunning scenery, talented crew, outstanding studio space and funding support we've got it all – including up to 10% grant incentive on top of the UK tax credit offer for qualifying animation projects.

Find out how Creative Wales can support your project: **creative.wales**

Bomper Studio

bomper studio

PRYDERIOUS

It's Africa's Time

Steve Rock, Storytelling Specialist

There is a multitude of wonderful children's characters originating from the African continent, excellently written, designed and beautifully produced. But, sadly, you will never see them.

Why? Well, there are a few reasons, ranging from you not looking in the right places to the product not being deemed worthy for traditional Western markets. When it comes to the African continent, there is still a line of thought that anything made there is simply for the people who live there.

This could not be further from the truth.

In 2020, Europe ranked as the leading destination for African migrants outside of Africa. Around 11 million African-born migrants lived in European countries that year. Nearly five million Africans resided in Asia, while about three million lived in North America. Overall, more than 19.5 million Africans were living in different world regions as of 2020.

Africa has a population of around 1.2 billion. In 2022, children younger than 15 accounted for 42% of the inhabitants. Without a doubt, Africa has a young population and, as technological innovation takes hold, there will be a change in not only how content is consumed, but *what* content is consumed.

At the time of writing, there is a lack of global representation for African children's content worldwide. The smart money is on this changing, sooner rather than later. In this piece I will touch upon some of the great work that's being created and provide some reasons to think differently about all the commercial and creative possibilities for the African children's market.

But first, full disclosure: I am not African – meaning, I was not born on the magnificent continent. I was born in sunny Tottenham, London. (No comments about the football team, please.) I reside in Cape Town and my young family is African; well, South African. Which makes me a foreigner in my own home.

And, like most children, mine consume a lot of media. One day while watching them, two thoughts presented themselves:

1. What they were watching wasn't created by people like them.
2. The content didn't reflect any aspect of who they were (West Indian, African or British).

While some of you may see nothing wrong with this, I choose to.

What's the 'cost' to children's young minds if they continually consume content from people who don't share their backgrounds or are from different environments? And, from a global perspective, what is the world missing out on if we simply keep promoting and consuming content from the more accepted traditional markets? In 2024, surely we need to expand representation on a global scale.

I grew up in a time and space where representation was sparse, be that at school or on television. Being Black was a rather shallow pool. You were either from "Africa" (that reasonably large place with 54 countries) or, and this is a quote, "…from that place Bob Marley comes from".

When I hear children assuming the actions, language patterns and fashion from North America, it made me question things: Why do so many parts of the world happily accept one culture as the gold standard? Should my children, who have never experienced that culture in person, be sounding like them?

For me, the answer to the second part of the question is a resounding "no".

So, with that in mind, I created a platform that offers 'local' content where they can hear (and in time, see) themselves, helping to normalise their voices in a regional and global context. And, surprise, surprise, I was far from the only one on this journey. It wasn't just me who was seeking to create and promote local content, and, more importantly, there is evidence that it's also being consumed.

Out of Tanzania there is Ubongo, a non-profit social enterprise that creates fun, localised and multi-platform educational content. By 2030 they aim to have 120 million children learning with them. Currently, Ubongo content is regularly viewed and listened to by 24 million learners across 63 TV stations and 21 radio stations.

In Nigeria there is Limitless Studios that produces *OmoBerry*, a commercial venture that at the time of writing has 312,000 subscribers. *OmoBerry* leverages high quality 3D animation and music to produce diverse and inclusive content for young audiences across the globe.

These are just two examples of very different models, finding a previously underserved audience.

So, in what ways can we realise the value of this potentially huge emerging market? Let's take a quick look at another, previously undervalued market.

The African continent, according to the World Economic Forum, is the world leader in digital banking. Now, while this may seem counter intuitive, let's take a closer look into why.

> "In Africa and many other developing markets, most digital banking takes the form of mobile banking. This is due to a lack of fixed communications infrastructure for wired internet access. Around three-quarters of online traffic in Africa goes via mobile phones, according to African Business.
>
> The GSM Association, which represents mobile network operators worldwide, ranks Sub-Saharan Africa as the world leader in mobile banking in terms of live services, subscribers and transactions."
> World Economic Forum

While the West invested heavily in fixed infrastructure, businesses realised that repeating the fixed communications model wasn't required in Africa, as they could utilise and build services around what swathes of the continent already had: mobile phones.

What I'm proposing is a greater use of innovation and free thinking to look at how best to co-create and promote content from the continent. We can all too easily get caught in following old models that worked for a particular time and space. We are living in such a fast-moving environment and we should look to create new models designed to support the production and promotion of content from emerging markets.

The quality of questions we ask ourselves will dictate the quality of answers. What you look for you will surely find. So, let's stop looking for or rehashing old stories, or reasons why things can't or won't work and figure out *how* we can make something work.

Let's find ways to develop strategic partnerships to meet a common goal; open our minds to finding new methods to engage with our market; offer true value for all stakeholders.

Asking a commissioning editor for a bag of cash isn't the way forward and while budgets may be shrinking, our ability to innovate isn't. Conversely, broadcasters and established production companies should not simply look to exploit creators and seek to retain the large piece of the ownership pie, simply because that's how it was done in the good old days. Times have and will continue to change and we all need to change with it.

I'm not saying it will be easy, but, in time, it will be worth it. After all, unexplored markets rarely stay unexplored for long.

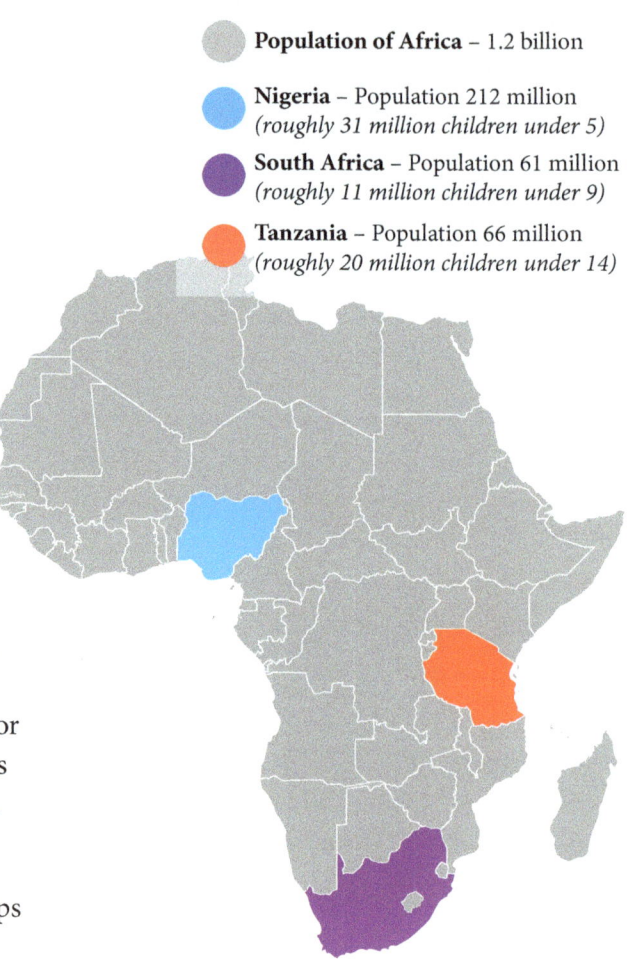

● **Population of Africa** – 1.2 billion

● **Nigeria** – Population 212 million
(roughly 31 million children under 5)

● **South Africa** – Population 61 million
(roughly 11 million children under 9)

● **Tanzania** – Population 66 million
(roughly 20 million children under 14)

Africa is the continent with the largest children's population.

The United Nations projects that by 2050, Africa's population will reach close to 2.5 billion. Such a figure would mean that more than 25 percent of the world's population will be African.

"No force on earth can stop an idea whose time has come." – Victor Hugo

It's Africa's time.

Larrikins And Lighthouses:
A Time Of Change In Australian Children's Television

Dr Liam Burke, Associate Professor of Screen Studies, Swinburne University of Technology and
Dr Joanna McIntyre, Senior Lecturer in Media Studies, Swinburne University of Technology

In 2024 the Australian High Commissioner to the UK, Stephen Smith, bestowed a special award for cultural impact on the children's show *Bluey* (2018–). The unprecedented honour recognised the animated series as a global phenomenon, but the success of *Bluey* belies how technological and legislative changes are creating uncertainty in the Australian children's television sector. Since 2021, our research project, Australian Children's Television Cultures (ACTC), has been investigating the roles and value of Australian children's television. For more than half a century, Australian children's television has been a cornerstone of Australian culture and vital to explorations and formulations of Australian national identity, but we've undertaken this research because Australian children's television is facing a silent crisis that is too big for one little blue dog to shoulder alone.

When the Australian High Commission bestowed its honour on *Bluey*, Smith described the show as a "fantastic cultural ambassador for Australia", adding "it allows modern day Australian stories to be taken to the world". For the uninitiated, *Bluey* is the Emmy Award-winning cartoon about a family of anthropomorphised Australian cattle dogs and that has become a ratings phenomenon since it first aired on Australia's main public service broadcaster, the ABC, in 2018. After years working in the UK on children's shows like *Charlie and Lola*, Australian animator Joe Brumm created *Bluey* as an Aussie response to *Peppa Pig*. *Bluey* follows the eponymous six year old Blue Heeler, her younger sister, Bingo, and their playful parents, Bandit and Chilli, in relatable, but always entertaining, family adventures. Parents, critics, and education experts around the world celebrate this heart-warming series for highlighting the importance of play as well as its humorous tone and ambitious ideas. *Bluey* is produced by Ludo Studio, based in Brisbane, Queensland. The show is co-funded by the UK's BBC Studios, which also sells the show internationally, including to Disney where it has proven incredibly successful on Disney+. In the US, *Bluey* was second only to legal drama *Suits* in 2023 Nielsen streaming viewership.

Although the global reach of *Bluey* is unprecedented for an Australian children's television show, Australia has long been recognised as a global provider of quality children's content. Arguably this proud tradition began with the enduring hit *Skippy the Bush Kangaroo* in the 1960s. When government support for local productions improved in the 1990s, Australia produced many memorable children's shows, including the spooky comedy *Round the Twist*, which national and international audiences enthusiastically embraced. This beloved live action series features an 'ordinary' single-parent family who happen to live in a lighthouse that is frequently the site of supernatural shenanigans.

The Twist family, Round the Twist

More recent outstanding Australian contributions to the global market include *Dance Academy*, *Little Lunch*, and *InBESTigators*, which first reached international audiences through broadcast television and, more recently, video on demand. Meanwhile, *Bananas in Pyjamas* and *The Wiggles* remain perennial preschool favourites. Although beloved Australian children's shows cover a wide range of genres and production styles, they tend to have some distinctive characteristics that endear them to audiences. These qualities include unambiguously Australian settings, recognisable family and schoolyard dynamics, and a uniquely Aussie sense of humour that is often described as 'larrikin'. Considering the proven popularity of these traits, the success of *Bluey* maybe isn't such a surprise as it evokes all these endearing elements and now takes them to an even wider audience.

Bluey may be deceptively simple with its unpretentious premise and down-to-earth sensibility but it is, worryingly, a load-bearing pillar of contemporary Aussie children's television. One of the key aims of our ACTC research project is to help stakeholders like producers, government agencies, and educators navigate the current era of transformation in the television industries. As a country with an enormous landmass but a small population, Australia's screen industries have survived and thrived because of federal government funding and legislation that protected them. It is with this assistance that Australian children's television was able to flourish. However, like many overseas equivalents, local Australian children's content producers have been struggling to find a way through the contemporary period of intense technological change in which video on demand has fundamentally altered viewing habits. In 2020, the Australian federal government used the changing television landscape as their rationale for removing long standing Australian children's content quotas. For decades these quotas had required commercial broadcasters to produce minimum amounts of Australian children's television and as such had safeguarded this small but influential sector. Within a few short years of losing these protections, the production and broadcast of Australian children's content has substantially declined, with the Australian Communications and Media Authority tracking how Australian children's content on commercial broadcasters dropped by 84% between 2019 and 2022.

The findings and outcomes of our project are designed to inform the Australian children's television sector as it navigates an era of increased viewing options, policy changes and new viewing practices. Our findings have been used in many policy submissions and discussion papers by our industry partner, the Australian Children's Television Foundation (ACTF), on topics ranging from School Refusal to subscription video on demand (SVOD) quotas and a new Prominence Framework for Smart TVs designed to increase the discoverability of local content. As part of this project, we are conducting a four-year programme of audience research with Australian parents and legal guardians of children aged 14 and younger to track and examine the viewing habits of Australian households with young children. We have discovered what Australian families tend to perceive as 'good' children's television, how children use different screen media platforms at home, and what value Australians place on children's content being 'local'.

Television industry scholar Anna Potter has examined the role of local children's content in the state's national agenda.[1] Parents also identified this nation-building function with a typical parent comment in our surveys stating that "[local children's TV] leans into our unique heritage without alienating those who have other experiences. Teaching about what it means to be Australian without creating a firm definition". However, Potter goes on to identify how the production of children's content in Australia is dependent on overseas funding through co-productions and international sales, which often means that only a small subset of the audience for successful Australian children's television shows is actually Australian. The perceived tensions between national cultural imperatives and global market forces have only been exacerbated by the dominance of global streaming services, which often fund or acquire shows on a worldwide basis. This transnational screen traffic prompts the question: is there still a need for shows that reflect a local experience? We investigated this issue in our research, asking parents and guardians how important they think it is that children's television is Australian: a large majority of our respondents (83%) deemed it important that the television their children watch is Australian.

Having established there is a consensus that local children's television is vital to Australian culture, we asked our hundreds of respondents to

---

[1] Potter, A. (2021) . Globalising the local in children's television for the post-network era: How Disney+ and BBC Studios helped Bluey the Australian cattle dog jump the national fence. In: *International journal of cultural studies*, 24(2).

describe what qualities they think make 'good' Australian children's shows and content. The most common response was that these shows were relatable, meaning they feature Australian accents, settings and iconography, as well as 'warts-and-all' portrayals of family life (often contrasted with 'overly sanitised' US shows). As one respondent emphasised, "Australian children need Australian shows". Another explained: "It's nice for children to see familiar landmarks and have issues that are current to them, as opposed to *Peppa Pig* and needing to explain why we don't have snow at Christmas".

The ways Aussie children's television is seen to contribute to nation building was revealed to be much more than a prescriptive or neo-colonial project. Notably, our research confirmed the indispensable roles of contemporary children's shows that prioritise respectful and authentic representations of First Nations people. For Indigenous and non-Indigenous children in Australia, live action children's shows *Thalu*, *Red Dirt Riders*, and *Barrumbi Kids*, and animated shows *Little J & Big Cuz* and *Eddie's Lil' Homies* offer thoughtful and engaging stories about Aboriginal and Torres Strait Islander people and knowledges, which are powerful components to Australian screen culture. Furthermore, Australia is a nation in which 30% of the population was born overseas, and parents who participated in our research celebrated how Australian children's television can provide a welcoming window into local culture for new Australians. For example, one father-of-two originally from Mexico described how the school-set mockumentary *Little Lunch* helped him and his children understand how the Australian education system works. For this family, and many others, a local

Fantasy series Thalu

show made school feel more 'familiar', offering a sense of comfort and empowerment to both parents and children.

From the lighthouse of *Round the Twist* to the larrikin humour of *Bluey*, local children's television is undoubtedly a social glue that connects Australians, communicating Australian identity and values to those within the nation, and to the world. However, with protections for the Australian children's television sector disappearing and more changes to the television industries still ahead, it remains to be seen where the next *Bluey* will come from.

> *Australian Children's Television Cultures (ACTC) is a research group based at Swinburne University of Technology. In partnership with the Australian Children's Television Foundation (ACTF) and RMIT University, ACTC is undertaking a four-year project (2021–2024) to investigate the roles of Australian children's television and other children's screen entertainment in people's lives, memories, families, and education.*
> *https://www.actcresearch.com/*

Children's Television For **Intercultural Dialogue:** *La Lleva*

Dr Enrique Uribe-Jongbloed, Cardiff University and Universidad Externado de Colombia

One child from one part of the country gets to visit another child living in another; they befriend and learn about the local culture through the experience of taking part in activities with their new friend. That was the main idea behind the reality TV show *La Lleva* (2010), which was produced for public service broadcasting in Colombia. It received many local and international accolades, leading to the commissioning of a second season. This second season changed its name to *La Lleva Internacional* (2012) and was developed as a co-production between four Latin American countries: the Dominican Republic, Mexico, Argentina and Colombia. Both seasons of the show are currently available on RTVCPlay, the Colombian national broadcaster's catch-up and streaming service, which does not impose any geo-localisation restriction to the show.

La Lleva based on a traditional children's game of the same name, known in English as 'It' or 'Tag', where one child chases other kids and, once able to touch one of them, calls "Tag, you're it" and then it is the other child's turn to chase others to tag them. Similarly, the show presents a kid travelling from one part of the country to another one and visits another child of the same age. The host then takes the visitor to experience the sights, traditions and everyday activities of their general area and culture, with the highlight always being something unique and special for the child. At the end of the show, the visitor passes on the 'Tag' to the host child, and they become the visitor of the next show.

Both the premise and the specific situations seen throughout the series make one thing clear: children are telling their story. It is their experience we share, and they present the world as they see it and enjoy it. Adults are seen only in the background, and they only come to the fore if the children want to present their connection to that adult as something relevant for their life or to present to their new friend. Visually, all shots are levelled at the children's height and their interactions and participation are, mostly, unmediated by adults.

Apart from its focus on the children's point of view, the show is also unique in that it portrays the diversity of Colombian nations, groups and languages. These characteristics turn a reality TV format, often associated with mindless entertainment, into a production that highlights how children engage with each other without discrimination, embrace and enjoy diversity, exhibit empathy and establish ties with one another, despite cultural, traditional and linguistic differences.

The show is presented in Spanish, with subtitles accompanying most of the voiced content spoken by the children in languages other than Spanish. However, some dialogue or interactions remains in the languages used by the participating children. The original Colombian version included different minority languages: Wayuunaiki, the largest indigenous language spoken in Colombia, with around 400,000 speakers; Ri-palenque (Palenquero), an endangered Spanish-based creole language with less than 500 living speakers; and Romani (Vlax), a Roma language whose speaker population in Colombia is of uncertain size.

The first season of the show was originally developed through financing made available by the Communication Department of Colombia's Ministry of Culture. It has been praised by academics and critics alike, and the fact that it was developed based on research about children's TV consumption carried out by the Ministry of Culture has been considered central to its success. The second season was financed in co-production between RTVC, the Colombian public service broadcaster, Paka-Paka, the Argentinian public children's TV channel, Canal 44 in Guadalajara, Mexico and Funglode in the Dominican Republic.

Claudia Bautista Arias, who was a member of the format development team and coordinator of content for international co-production in the second season, has called it a life-changing experience, personally and professionally, because "the original design of the series [...] was centred wholly in the fact that children are not only consumers of audiovisual discourses, but can also be protagonists without being instrumentalised by adults". This is something that is made evident in the 'format bible' – which describes how the non-scripted show should focus on the children's perspectives, emotions and interests. As opposed to adult reality shows, the conflict that raises emotions in the audience should be centred in discovery and surprise, rather than on confrontation and opposition. The bible elaborates on the process of selecting children for participation, the types of questions and the way to ask them – not prompting children to react in a certain manner or allowing adults to intervene unless invited by the children. When carrying out the international co-production, local crews undertook the production, ensuring cultural understanding and preventing exoticism, and enabling children to present their own culture in a way that suited them.

La Lleva is a prime example of good quality children's television that has managed to have an international impact, providing evidence of the potential of the often-derided reality TV format. It has also expanded to become a useful educational tool for children on topics of intercultural dialogue and tolerance, and RTVC offers guides and other materials to use its content for educational purposes in schools. However, in terms of audience numbers, it really did not live up to the quality of its content, due to the low uptake of public broadcast television in Colombia. The reflection here is about the impact and reach of quality children's television. Hopefully, *La Lleva* will eventually reincarnate as a format elsewhere, and its intercultural potential will be explored and shared by many more children.

©Image by starline on Freepik

Pocoyó As A Spanish–British Cultural Milestone

Silvia Rusiñol Romero, Doctoral Researcher, Universidad de Sevilla

Set within a lively and welcoming atmosphere, the 3D animation show *Pocoyó* follows the adventures of a preschooler who is constantly discovering the world, interacting with it alongside his friends Pato, Elly, Loula, and Pajaroto. Each episode presents simple, yet engaging scenarios designed to encourage children to explore and learn about colours, numbers, shapes and basic social interactions.

Beginning its broadcast on ITV in the UK in 2005, *Pocoyó* quickly gained global acclaim. Produced by Zinkia Entertainment, a Spanish animation studio, the first two seasons were co-produced in collaboration with Granada Films and the initial season with Cosgrove Hall Films, both UK-based production companies.

Guillermo García, one of the creators of the series, had two distinct objectives while developingt of the initial idea. Firstly, there was a deliberate effort to reflect the genuine experiences of childhood, prioritising spontaneity and naturalness over idealised portrayals. Secondly, there was a conscious intention to create a humorous yet educational cartoon, drawing inspiration from the timeless charm of Charlie Chaplin's work but crafted specifically for young audiences. This innovative approach embodied the trend of 'edutainment', which attempts to blend educational value with entertainment content. By embracing this approach, 'óyó' offers a captivating viewing experience that engages children while subtly imparting valuable lessons.

Pocoyó statue in Léon, Spain

What makes Pocoyó, *Pocoyó*?

Pocoyó incorporates three distinctive elements that have made it quite unique:

1. **Visual minimalism:** Pocoyó's visual world is characterized by simplicity and clarity, with its white background serving as a canvas for vibrant, colorful characters. This design choice ensures the characters' prominence and enhances visual engagement. While some may speculate that budget considerations drove this decision, it wasn't the only factor at play. The creators wanted *Pocoyó* to look different from other shows like *Teletubbies*, so they used a simple white background to make it stand out visually.
2. **Narrative guidance:** Central to the series' storytelling is the presence of a narrator that serves as a guiding voice throughout each episode. The narrator not only provides context and commentary but also facilitates understanding by framing the narrative and reinforcing key messages. This narrative approach draws inspiration from the 60s cartoon *The Pink Panther* (1963), which similarly employed a narrator to enrich the storytelling.
3. **Conflict resolution:** The television program typically follows a familiar conflict resolution structure, wherein characters encounter challenges or dilemmas that require resolution. Initially, the British production partners emphasised the importance of portraying *Pocoyó* facing consequences for his actions, rather than simply misbehaving.

The door opened

The children's television channel Clan TV was officially launched in 2005 as part of the Spanish public broadcaster RTVE (Radiotelevisión Española). A year after its debut in the UK, *Pocoyó* made its way to Spanish screens through this channel, quickly becoming one of its most beloved series. Although it was primarily produced by Zinkia Entertainment in Spain, it benefited from collaboration with British companies during its early seasons, marking it as one of the initial co-productions integrated into Spain's public television catalogue for kids.

Since then, international co-production agreements have played a crucial role in the growth and development of Spain's audiovisual industry. According to Pumares & Fontaine (2021), European TV animation

© Chaquetadepollo.

co-productions contribute to 36% of all TV animation hours produced in Spain, over 50% of content on its public children's channel is the result of co-productions and the acquisition of foreign productions. These agreements have become vital for securing extra funding, distributing costs and risks, utilising incentives from multiple countries and expanding into wider markets. Moreover, the European Convention on Cinematographic Co-production has facilitated multilateral production ventures, enabling collaborations with countries like the UK, leaders in the animation sector. Notable examples include feature films like *Planet 51* (2009), as well as television series like *Bradley and Bee* (2018).

Universally loved, socially relevant, technologically advanced

For almost 20 years *Pocoyó* has been captivating and inspiring thousands of young viewers. Its success lies in several key factors that are still evident in today's productions:

- **Universality:** The program is widely appealing and timeless, transcending specific cultural or geographical boundaries. It exists in an imaginary fictional space accessible to all.

- **Addressing important themes:** The show effectively tackles significant topics like friendship, problem-solving, tolerance, respect and diversity in ways that children can easily understand. This commitment to exploring deeper social themes has continued in newer productions, aiming not just to entertain but also to educate and foster positive values.

- **Technological innovation:** The animation techniques used in *Pocoyó*, such as the use of CGI (Computer Generated Imagery) and 3D animation, have set a standard for visual quality.

Beyond *Pocoyó*: what is next?

Since *Pocoyó* first aired, the way we watch shows has changed a lot, especially with the rise of streaming platforms like YouTube, Netflix or Disney+. This shift has reshaped how content is produced and distributed. The most notable change is how these platforms, often acting as distributors, now make it easier for children's programs to reach global audiences, potentially fostering collaborations between countries to create content with international appeal. In this context, one of the latest co-productions between Spain and the UK, *Bad Dinosaurs* (2024–), distributed by Netflix, shows the enduring value of UK–Spain co-production.

References

DIBOOS, Federación de Animación. (2018). *Libro Blanco. La industria española de la animación y los efectos visuales.* https://spainaudiovisualhub.mineco.gob.es/content/dam/seteleco-hub-audiovisual/resources/pdf/DIBOOS_LIBRO%20BLANCO_Sep2018.pdf

Pumares, M.J. and Fontaine, G. (December, 2021). *Animation films and TV series in Europe Key figures.* European Audiovisual Observatory.

The Power Of Representation:
Children Who Migrate

Jana Navarria, Writer and TV Script Executive, **Makaela Lewis**, Programme Coordinator, Media Movers, Heard and **Zoë Speekenbrink**, Senior Programme Manager, Media Movers, Heard

"When I see myself represented on screen I feel the joy of being seen and that people know I am here and matter. We need stories that do this more and we need them to drown out the negativity." – Precious, network member of Media Movers, Heard

Precious is a young person with a migrant background who moved to the UK with her family when she was three years old. Her words illustrate just how personal the media is – it's a mirror to our lives, a way for us to be recognised and feel included and valued in the world. Alongside this, and perhaps most importantly, media is a powerful force that has the very real ability to influence public perception. Sharing stories invites people to come along on a journey, to connect with those they're seeing on screen and to solidify or form new opinions based on the information they're receiving. Often in the media, stories of people with migrant backgrounds are one-dimensional, brief and can inadvertently 'other' those who migrate, reducing them to stereotypes or negative portrayals, when this isn't the reality. People with migrant backgrounds aren't the sum of the small parts we typically see on screen; they're people like everyone else, sharing in the same joys and heartaches, losses and successes. It's crucial then, that we portray those who migrate, and their stories, authentically in order to capture the nuance, diversity and richness of their experiences. In doing so, and as Precious says, good representation can drown out the bad.

If we look at children's media, stories about children and families from migrant backgrounds seem to be few and far between. This is surprising considering that in the UK, more than a quarter of children under the age of 18 have at least one parent born abroad,[1] and in the year ending September 2022, there were over 5,000 applications for asylum made by unaccompanied children.[2] On top of this, current world events mean that migration will soon become the norm rather than something reserved

---

[1] Briefing: Children of Migrants in the UK, published by The Migration Observatory at The University of Oxford, 2022
[2] Data published by The Refugee Council

for a minority of people. Given there are so many children who have lived experience of migration in some form or another, content that focuses on their stories is not only current but necessary.

Understandably, telling good migration stories may feel like a confusing or weighty topic to present to a young audience. There may be uncertainty over whose story to tell and how to tell it, as well as worry over how the content will be received. At Heard, a charity that supports the media to tell better stories about marginalised groups, we've developed key guidelines to help frame migration in a way that is meaningful and appropriate for young audiences. These guidelines are the outcome of consultations with a group of young people in our network who have lived experience of migration, extensive research into best practice communications and our experience working closely with writers, production companies, commissioners, broadcasters and streaming services. It is our aim that in making available these guidelines, we can support media professionals in telling more authentic and nuanced stories on migration.

Guidelines to tell impactful migration stories in children's content

1. Portray children with migrant backgrounds so that migration alone doesn't define them.

When creating children's content about migration, it's important to focus stories beyond the stereotype and steer away from showing 'sad' experiences or content solely about the migration journey. Repeatedly telling emotionally intense, traumatic or negative stories can further solidify inaccurate perceptions of those who migrate and have a detrimental impact on children with migrant backgrounds watching. Of course, this isn't to say we should shy away completely from depicting this part of someone's experience but it should be balanced with other areas of life such as relationships, school, family and friendships. Elements of migration will naturally be built into the make-up of a character and inform their personality, behaviours and actions. This makes for a multi-layered character who is not simply defined by their experience or identity as a 'migrant'. Embedding the nuances of having a migrant background into everyday experiences is also a much more effective way of engaging audiences, especially younger ones.

This is exemplified in *Phoenix Rise* (2023–), a programme where six teens learn that the only way to survive school is by sticking together. One of the main characters is Rani, whose parents are political refugees from Iraq and who now live in Coventry. While this experience informs Rani's personality through the ways in which her parents guide her, it's not the totality of who she is; her parents' migration story doesn't define her solely. Instead, Rani is someone who is quiet but fierce in her own thoughtful way, a dreamer with aspirations of being on stage, a loyal friend who'd do anything for her mates, hardworking with a strong moral compass, and a girl who's dipping her toe in the dating pool while navigating mainstream high school. Through all of this, Rani has the support of her friends and, while her storyline in series 1 and 2 deals with elements of being a child of migrants, it never feels as though this defines Rani's character entirely.

2. Contextualise and show the bigger picture.

While it's important to depict personal and individual stories, it's also beneficial to root these within a wider context to help audiences understand the systems and processes in which migration occurs. By doing this, it takes away the onus on the individual (ie. the idea that "they got themselves into this situation and it's rare this happens") and places the emphasis on circumstances, policies and structures of government, highlighting the hostility of the migration system. This helps educate young audiences on the bigger picture while also reaffirming the experiences of children with migrant backgrounds who are watching. While on the surface this may seem complex to portray, it doesn't necessarily need to be done in a heavy handed way. Widening the lens and providing context can be achieved through a conversation or a brief moment in the plot.

In *The Dumping Ground* (2013–), there are several storylines where young migrants, who have been forced to flee their home countries, have arrived at the children's care home. As the other children piece together the backstories of the new arrivals – how and why they're now in the UK – we get an understanding of the bigger picture: the newly arrived children didn't flee because they were 'naughty' or 'bad'; they were forced due to circumstance and had no other choice. Through understanding the context, the children in the care home can sympathise and rally around their new friends. Importantly, this gives viewers a roadmap of behaviour to emulate.

3. Portray young people with migrant backgrounds just like everyone else.

While many people with migrant backgrounds have excelled and achieved success in various fields, it's important to also show the stories of

The Dumping Ground

ordinary people. This helps young audiences relate to what they're watching and, specifically, helps children with migrant backgrounds feel included when they see their everyday lives reflected on screen. In this way, celebrating the average individual doing interesting things is just as significant as shining a spotlight on stories of achievement. Children, whatever their background, also don't exist in a vacuum. Similar to the first guideline, portraying stories where young people with migrant backgrounds are active parts of communities, peer groups and wider families make for relatable characters. Equally, using imagery that is warm and human helps young viewers relate to the character at the centre of the story and, through that, helps them better understand their experiences of migration.

Mirabel, the lead character in *Encanto*'s (2021) story of a displaced family in Colombia, is the only family member without a 'gift' – she's ordinary and relatable, and it's only at the end of the film that she realises her gift is being herself. *Encanto* shows audiences the power that exists within every person, reminding the viewer that everyone is special in their own way. It also highlights the pressures that many young people of migrant backgrounds may experience in feeling the need to be 'extraordinary'. In addition, the film highlights the power of community and supporting each other, and the magic that comes with accepting and welcoming others into our lives.

4. Show there's more than one experience of migration.

There are many experiences of migration that often don't get seen. By only portraying one type of journey, migration is reduced to tropes and stereotypes that have the consequence of giving audiences a narrow view of the migration experience. To avoid this, show diverse stories that highlight the various ways people move and the reasons behind why they have had to migrate. The examples drawn from *Phoenix Rise*, *The Dumping Ground* and *Encanto* illustrate this guideline well – migration is different for each of the central characters and their families. By presenting different stories, unique migration experiences can be brought to life and show an audience there's not only one journey that children and families take.

As these four key guidelines demonstrate, there are ways in which stories about children and families who migrate can be communicated to a young audience appropriately whilst capturing real-life experiences that are nuanced and varied. The examples we've provided from existing children's content also show how elements of migration can add a richness to many different stories and help to create complex, well-rounded and interesting characters, which reflect the lived experience of thousands of children who migrate to the UK each year. As such, these programmes set the benchmark for good migration portrayal.

Ultimately, there is a place for migration stories in children's content. Not only is it important to educate young audiences on their peers who may have migrated, but it's crucial that every child sees themselves represented on screen. As one of our network members, Isabel, says, "I see myself on the screen as a free, happy, funny and enjoyable person." With this in mind, let's continue to find ways in which we can tell authentic and diverse stories of migration within children's content.

ORIEL SQUARE

Defining and delivering the best in educational products and services

 **STRATEGIC PLANNING**

 **COMMUNICATIONS**

 **IMPLEMENTATION**

 Oriel Square Limited   www.orielsquare.co.uk

Can We **Normalise Children's Rights** Through Children's Media?

Dr Dawn Watkins, Professor of Law, University of Sheffield

In 2012, I was teaching undergraduate law students about the United Nations Convention on the Rights of the Child (UNCRC) and the wide range of rights this international treaty affords to children and young people in the UK, when news broke of the death of four year old Daniel Pelka, who had been abused and eventually murdered by his mother and her partner. Daniel was being beaten and starved at home and had been looking in the bins at school for food. Yet the serious case review that followed his death reported there was no record of anyone talking directly to Daniel about his life at home or the reasons for his apparent hunger (Coventry LSCB, 2013). For me, his story represented an unbearable example of how the right of a child to be protected from harm under the UNCRC, and by domestic law, is not being realised in practice. It also raised the question of how a young child like Daniel, whose experiences may seem 'normal' to them, might come to realise they are suffering abuse, and seek help. Or in other words, how does a child or young person know when a problem is a problem?

Research in the field of human rights education (HRE) tells us that through learning about rights and reflecting on their own situations, children and young people can become aware of injustices they are experiencing in their everyday lives and seek help, or act themselves to change things for the better (Bajaj et al., 2016). This provides hope. However, the *Law in Children's Lives* study I led from 2014–16 demonstrated that the state of 'everyday' legal knowledge among children was a cause for concern. In this study of over 600 children in England aged 8–11 years, *no* child referred to their rights under the UNCRC (Watkins et al., 2018). More recently, a report from the Committee on the Rights of the Child (CtRC) has also noted 'with concern' the relatively low level of knowledge regarding the UNCRC among adults, children and young people in the UK, and recommends the adoption of a national strategy for raising children's rights awareness among the population (CtRC, 2023).

Perhaps the most obvious way to address this gap in knowledge among children and young people is through learning in schools. The UK government has been advised to consider introducing human rights-focused 'civic and constitutional' education into schools (The Independent Human Rights Act Review, 2021) and the Welsh Government has introduced a duty on schools to adopt a human rights approach to the design and delivery of the curriculum (Curriculum and Assessment (Wales) Act 2021). This is encouraging, but the relatively recent demise of citizenship education and research revealing hesitancy among teachers concerning the delivery of health and relationships education in schools (Struthers, 2020) suggests we may need to manage our expectations concerning the practical implementation of these 'in principle' recommendations.

So something else is needed. And arguably something that children and young people can access directly. My approach has been to explore ways in which we might be able to provide children and young people with opportunities to develop their legal knowledge, skills and confidence through game-based learning. The *Law in Children's Lives* study involved the creation of a digital gamified survey called *Adventures with Lex*, where players encountered a range of law-related scenarios situated in four 'worlds' (the park, a shop, a friend's house and school), accompanied by a naïve alien. This proved to be a successful way to engage children in considering law-related issues, and provided proof of concept for project FORTITUDE, a five-year project funded by the European Research Council.

The principal aim of this project is to work with children and young people aged 3–15 years to create game-based interventions (digital and physical) that will both measure and improve their legal knowledge, skills and confidence, or 'legal capability'. We are collaborating with the Creative Technology team at Four, in Sheffield, to achieve this aim. The effectiveness of the main digital legal learning game is due to be evaluated across England in Autumn 2024, and we intend to make it more widely available to children and young people at the end of the project in May 2025. Ultimately, FORTITUDE aims to boost the legal capability of children internationally, by creating a specification through which the project's outputs can be adapted and developed in other populations.

If the aims of the project are successful, then we will have created opportunities for some children and young people to become more aware of their rights, more able to identify when a problem is a problem, and more confident to seek help. But much more remains to be done. Imagine a world where children and young people become more aware of their rights across the entire range of media they experience. Sonia Livingstone's *Children's Rights by Design* provides a significant step towards this, as it provides a framework for designers and innovators to respect and realise children's rights under the UNCRC when creating new content. But what if the UNCRC *is* the content, contextualised as part of the everyday stories of children's lives? Can we normalise children's rights through children's media?

References

Bajaj, M., Cislaghi, B. and Mackie, G. (2016). Advancing Transformative human rights education, Appendix D to the *Report of the Global Citizenship Commission*. New York: Open Book.

Committee on the Rights of the Child, Concluding Observations on the combined sixth and seventh periodic reports of the UK, 22 June 2023, CRC/C/GBR/CO/6-7.

Coventry LSCB, Final Overview Report of Serious Case Review re Daniel Pelka (September 2013).

Struthers, A.E.C. (2020). *Teaching human rights in primary schools: Overcoming the barriers to effective practice.* Abingdon, UK: Routledge.

Watkins, D., Lai-Chong Law, E., Barwick, J. and Kirk, E. (2018). Exploring children's understanding of law in their everyday lives, in *Legal Studies* 38(1), (2018), pp.59–78.

Paying Attention: Is Toddler Attention Shaped By Early Media Exposure?

Dr Tim Smith, Professor of Cognitive Data Science, Creative Computing Institute, University of the Arts London, **Dr Rachael Bedford**, Professor of Biological and Experimental Psychology, Queen Mary University of London, **Claire Essex**, Centre for Brain and Cognitive Development, Birkbeck, University of London and **Dr Hannah Pickard**, Centre for Brain and Cognitive Development, Birkbeck, University of London

The intensity of toddler screen exposure is increasing year on year. UK children watch on average 9.6 hours of broadcast TV or on demand video per week with the majority of toddlers using touchscreens daily. The sensory–cognitive stimulation provided by screens far exceeds that of reality, potentially shaping cognition during a child's first few years, when brain development is at its peak. Concerned parents, policymakers and scientists have long questioned the potential impact of screen time on young children's cognitive development, with some authorities recommending strict time limits for toddler media use. But such recommendations often fail to appreciate the potential educational benefits of age-appropriate content designed with child development in mind.

A particular concern for parents is how screen exposure may impact developing attention skills. Attention control (ie. learning to control what we focus our brain's limited cognitive resources on) develops rapidly during the first few years of life and plays an important role in how a child learns to regulate their behaviours and emotions; skills that are critical for later education. Many studies looking at the association with early screen media exposure have reported greater attentional problems in children who have more screen time. Although associations are often moderated by a family's socioeconomic background, parenting styles and the educational nature of the content being presented, researchers propose that such associations come about because screen media is designed to make all viewers attend to content in the same way, maximising the automatic pull of attention to the screen and minimising the need for viewers to voluntarily decide where to look. Spending too much time in an automatic attention mode during toddlerhood may limit opportunities to practice and develop more deliberate control, leading to attention problems in later childhood.

But what evidence supports this, and what does it mean for media creators?

Directing attention

Eye-tracking, which can record how children shift their eyes and attention over time, has shown how infant attention progresses from being predominantly under automatic control, attracted to prominent visual details like motion in the first few months of life, to being increasingly under voluntary control as the child learns to direct attention to points of interest such as faces and objects (see Figure 1). Children's media must accommodate immature attention by guiding the young viewer towards critical scene details (eg. a speaking character). When it does so, screen media can maximise toddler attention and aid learning. However, too much direction towards cognitively challenging content during viewing may have consequences after viewing.

Disengaging from a screen

Any parent of a toddler will be familiar with the tantrums and hyperactivity that may erupt immediately after the screen is switched off. Several studies have investigated this spill-over effect and shown that screen content that is too intense or too fantastical for children can impair voluntary control of attention and as a result limit children's ability to regulate behaviours (Kostyrka-Allchorne et al., 2017). Not all content has the same depleting effect: four year old children performed worse on real-world attention control tasks after watching episodes of *SpongeBob SquarePants*, a fantastical kid's cartoon, than when they watched an educational show, *Caillou* (Lillard & Peterson 2011). TV shows that deplete attention control capacity tend to be more visually intense (Essex et al. 2022), but even when these visual differences are controlled, fantastical content still leads to poorer attentional control immediately after viewing.

Is there a longer term link between screen time and later attention control?

In 2015, we ran a lab study which followed infants over time, measuring screen use and developing attention control. Capitalising on the 'natural experiment' of whether parents chose to expose their infants to touchscreen devices (tablets and smartphones) or not, we recruited families into the Leverhulme

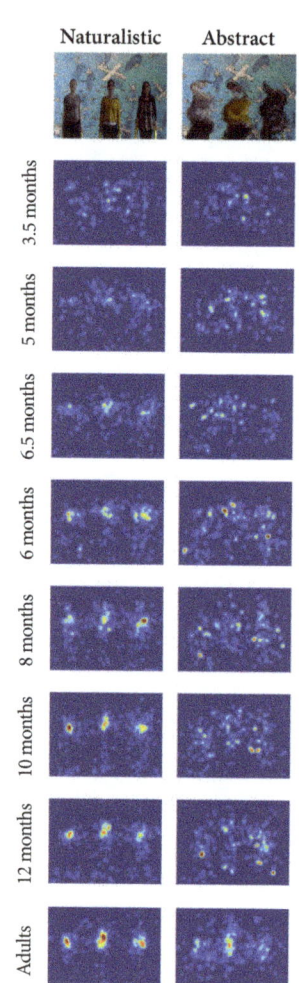

Figure 1: Heatmaps of infant (3.5 to 12 months of age) and adult gaze whilst watching videos of women performing child-friendly actions, eg. peak-a-boo (Naturalistic column) and scrambled versions of the same videos (Abstract column). Hotter colours indicate more frequent gaze in that screen location; cooler colours indicate more dispersed gaze. Notice how gaze is increasingly directed to faces across age in Naturalistic but not Abstract versions (except in adults). Taken from Haensel and colleagues (2016).

and Wellcome Trust-funded *Toddler Attentional Behaviours and Learning with Touchscreens* (TABLET) project. Infants were recruited based on whether their daily exposure to touchscreen devices was above (high users) or below (low users) the average at 12 months of age (ten minutes). By matching groups on background factors at 12 months, including child age, sex, family socioeconomic status, child IQ and temperament, we were able to ensure that the link between touchscreen use and attention findings was not driven by existing differences between families.

Toddlers completed eye-tracking tasks to measure attention control at 12 months, 18 months and 3.5 years. We found that high touchscreen users had faster automatic attention (eg. quicker to spot the odd-one-out) and showed some evidence of less voluntary attention control – they looked more towards a distractor that was not relevant for their task. This finding of reduced voluntary attention control was also reflected across several real-world and computer-based tasks at 3.5 years; the high users showed reduced working memory and less flexible switching between rules. This finding may be due to the child's broader media environment, rather than specific to touchscreen use, as it did not remain after controlling for TV viewing. The study's longitudinal design also allowed us to test whether early screen use predicted later attention differences. While we found evidence for concurrent associations between screen use and attention control, we did not find evidence for longitudinal effects. In other words, early screen use was not linked to later attention control, suggesting any short term effects of screen use on attention may not persist over time.

Does screen exposure *cause* attention differences?

We have shown that screen media can directly shape attention during viewing, have immediate spill-over effects after viewing and is associated with concurrent individual differences in attention. However, to show that screen exposure causes attention control to develop differently we need to account for screen exposure in randomly selected families, ie. conduct a randomised controlled trial (RCT).

In 2022 we began the first RCT of a Parent-Administered Screen Time Intervention (PASTI; funded by Nuffield Foundation). This trial aimed to look at whether removing screen time in the hour before bed improved toddler sleep and attention over seven weeks. We focussed on the hour before bed because a) there is global consensus on this recommendation (Royal College of Paediatrics and Child Health, 2019); and b) our conversations with early years practitioners and parents suggested that this change would be more feasible given the realities of modern family life. Over the course of a year, the families taking part reported finding it easy to stop their toddler seeing screens in the hour before bed and maintain this for most of the seven-week trial. Analysis of whether the intervention improved toddler attention and sleep is ongoing, but once available it will be the first time we will be able to say whether toddler screen media exposure is causing differences in attention.

The developmental science of early years media effects is an expanding area with many research questions still to be investigated. Based on the latest findings we'd like to make the following recommendations:

Researchers

- Co-create research questions with diverse parents and media creators to ensure research can maximise impact.
- Conduct more randomised controlled trials of early years media use to provide a strong evidence base that can inform policy and practice.
- Create better measures of the quality of content (ie. developmental appropriateness) and the context of viewing to move the field beyond 'quantity' measures of exposure.

Media creators

- Consider the flow of viewer attention through a show and whether the balance between moments that drive attention (eg. intense/exciting) and calmer, more thoughtful moments is right for your viewer age.
- Children are active viewers, even from a very young age. Give them opportunities to actively search for and discover things on the screen to keep them engaged and help learn attention control.
- Collaborate with developmental scientists to test your intuitions about how to optimally shape viewer attention.

You can find updates on the findings of the TABLET project at www.cinelabresearch.com.

References

Essex, C., Gliga, T., Singh, M. and Smith, T.J. (2022). Understanding the differential impact of children's TV on executive functions: a narrative-processing analysis. *Infant Behavior and Development 66*, ISSN 0163-6383.

Haensel, J., de Urabain, I.S., Senju, A., and Smith, T. (2016). Developmental changes in infants' attention to naturalistic faces and visual saliency. *Journal of Vision*, 16(12), 65–65.

Kostyrka-Allchorne, K., Cooper, N.R., and Simpson, A. (2017). The relationship between television exposure and children's cognition and behaviour: A systematic review. *Developmental Review*.

Lillard, A.S., and Peterson, J. (2011). The immediate impact of different types of television on young children's executive function. *Pediatrics*.

Viner, R., Davie, M., and Firth, A. (2019). The health impacts of screen time: a guide for clinicians and parents. *Edinburgh, Scotland: Royal College of Paediatrics and Child Health*.

Rethinking **Short-Form Media** For Generation Alpha

Dr Sonia Tiwari, Researcher, College of Education, Penn State University

Imagine a generation of children who are not just 'digital natives' but active consumers and co-creators of digital media even before they learn to read and write. Coined by social researcher Mark McCrindle, 'Generation Alpha' encompasses those born from 2010 through 2025. This generation doesn't stop at consuming media that was designed for them by adults – but co-design their own entertainment through building worlds, characters, stories, images, videos and other media afforded by the platforms and tools of their choice.

Gen Alpha's interaction with technology is instinctive, influencing their learning, entertainment and social interactions from a very young age. As the first generation entirely born into an age dominated by smartphones, social media, and advanced technology, Gen Alpha can teach content creators from prior generations how to rethink their traditionally prescriptive approach to children's media.

This generation's hallmark traits include a preference for visual and interactive content, a notable reduction in attention spans and an unparalleled familiarity with digital platforms. And what media category has visual and/or interactive content, is suitable for shorter attention spans and fits into a wide range of digital platforms? Short-form media!

Short-form media: then and now

Short-form media is not a novel concept. Its roots can be traced back to the most popular two word mashup in the children's media industry: edutainment. Series like *Sesame Street* masterfully combined education with entertainment in bite-sized segments. Interstitials on networks like PBS KIDS introduced brief, engaging content sandwiched between two longer episodes packaged in a 20–30 minute program. Nickelodeon's #kidstogether initiative showcased how short-form content could be utilised to educate and comfort young audiences about current events, such as the Covid-19 pandemic, through brief, engaging formats. These past examples underline the evolving nature of short-form media, setting the stage for today's platforms and content.

Platforms like TikTok, Snapchat, and YouTube Shorts dominate social media, illustrating the shift in media consumption towards quick, digestible content. Animated videos by TedEd, Oxford Sparks, Kurzgesagt and AsapScience are great examples of short-form educational content that supports 'microlearning' – delivering quick and simplified information for a specific learning outcome.

The brevity of content should not compromise its quality or message, demanding creativity from creators to make every second count. The caution here, though, is that while a minute of video can educate a child about science, the same minute can also deliver damaging information before a child can think and scroll away. Countries around the globe are rethinking laws around protecting children in a changing media landscape. There are currently, however, no clear guidelines about in-game media or AI-generated media (where it's easy to hide behind anonymity), and plenty of grey areas within existing media laws that should ideally protect children.

Photo by Laura Chouette on Unsplash

Ideas for evolving short-form media

While animated short films, short television episodes and mini-games have been around for decades, short-form media for Gen Alpha can take on other modalities. For example:

- **Social media reels** – Consider creating one-minute videos for social media giants such as YouTube and Instagram, with the opportunity to pair video content with text/captions. For example, the video could include a brief story or lesson, followed by activity prompts in the caption that may co-engage caregivers and educators with children.

- **Flash fiction** – For compressing great stories in short-form, seek inspiration from screenplays of past animated short-form series such as *Sesame Street* or the new PBS KIDS preschool series *Jelly, Ben &Pogo*. One can also seek inspiration from children's picture books capturing engaging tales with few words and great visuals. For Gen Alpha, these screenplays and stories can be revisited with a 'flash fiction' lens, compressing the typical story plot structure to the most important beats to the point where a full story can be understood within less than a minute on-screen, in audio or in a brief caption.

- **Transmedia suites** – Spread the engagement across multiple platforms, which may involve funneling one platform into another. For example, link a game on Roblox to a livestream on Twitch or a channel on YouTube, with links to an informational website with offline activities and other resources.

- **Co-created content** – Media consumption doesn't need to end with content produced by adults and prescribed to children. Gen Alpha kids can co-create their own content, given the tools and guidance to create something original. This may look like designing worlds in Roblox, remixing projects on Scratch, generating new stories on Story Spark using AI, or having an open-ended conversation with an animated AI character chatbot Furwee.
- **Mixing linear and non-linear** – In 2019, PBS KIDS collaborated with researchers at UC Irvine to explore how kids can interact with television characters using AI. Further development of this technology may soon allow kids to ask questions, act on activity prompts and engage with characters in television or streaming episodes in other unique ways. Linear media can be mixed and extended with non-linear interactions.
- **Phygital** – Consider combining physical products with digital short-form experiences. This may look like talking to a toy while reading a book with Readyland, building something new with LEGO bricks based on recommendations by the BrickIt app, playing a toy piano that corresponds to a mobile game by PlayShifu, or holding a MergeCube to inspect a planet up-close. Gen Alpha kids can blur the line between experiencing media physically and digitally.

The integration of AR/VR, voice recognition, generative AI and other interactivities present new avenues for engagement, blending entertainment with immersive learning experiences for children. The push towards user-generated content for kids and by kids signifies a shift towards more participatory media consumption for Gen Alpha.

Each generation's media consumption trends are defined by the context of the time: the living conditions, resources, technological advancements and affordances, notable events, culture and systemic challenges. Media is context-sensitive and we, as a collective of children's media professionals belonging to prior generations, may be stuck in a context-agnostic "We know what's good for kids" mindset unless we embrace Gen Alpha's uniqueness and meet them where they are.

References

McCrindle, Mark. "Generation Alpha Defined." McCrindle. https://mccrindle.com.au/insights/blogarchive/generation-alpha-defined/

"Creating Media to Meet the Information Needs of Children." Nieman Reports. https://niemanreports.org/articles/creating-media-to-meet-the-information-needs-of-children/

Xu, Y., Levine, J., Vigil, V., Ritchie, D., Zhang, S., Thomas, T., Barrera, C., Meza, M., Bustamante, A. S., & Warschauer, M. (2023). Interaction with a television character powered by artificial intelligence promotes children's science learning. Paper presented at the American Educational Research Association 2023. https://osf.io/preprints/edarxiv/m3ej9

Putting **Children's Wellbeing** At The Centre Of **Digital Play Design**

Dr Fiona Scott, Lecturer in Digital Literacies and Director, Literacies and Language Research Cluster, School of Education, University of Sheffield

Mainstream and scholarly discussions about children's digital play have, for a long time, focused primarily on the avoidance of possible harms. In recent years however, it has been common to see suggestions that digital play can be positive for children because certain types of digital play support their learning. Both are vital considerations and associated with important ongoing research. In contrast with children's play more broadly, however, there has historically been little consideration of how digital play might actually support children's wellbeing, a topic that is now attracting increasing popular and policy interest. The sheer amount of time that children spend playing in digital environments presents an opportunity for both policy makers and game designers to positively influence wellbeing. However, both parties need access to high quality, research-informed insights to guide their decision making.

That's exactly what I've had the privilege to be working on with a brilliant research team and wider project team over the last four years. The RITEC project (Responsible Innovation in Technology for Children) is a collaboration between internationally renowned academic researchers working across 17 countries, the child-rights organisation UNICEF, the LEGO Group and others, including children's play designers and the Joan Ganz Cooney Center. We share a desire to understand the relationship between children's digital play and their wellbeing and a shared goal to prioritise children's wellbeing in a digital age, helping both businesses and policymakers with the tools and knowledge to put wellbeing at the centre of design. The project team has undertaken literature reviews, meta-analyses and four substantial research projects all focused on this goal and we are now delighted to be sharing our insights.

My own contribution has been leading the family case study research at the University of Sheffield. Working with four experts in the UK, South Africa, Australia and Cyprus, I have led a research team of 21, working with 50 children aged 6–12 and their families across these four countries. We adopted a very in-depth approach, making between four to six visits to each family over a total period of 14 months to uncover the digital play choices and practices of children and families, as well as how these connected with their wellbeing. Across a total of 240 home visits, we spoke to children and their families, observed them in their everyday digital and non-digital play and asked them to take part in a range of research tasks and sharing of family-generated photographs and videos. Meanwhile, our sibling research project in New York (New York University and City University, New York) conducted a multi-week digital play intervention involving 255 children aged 8–12 in the US, Chile and South Africa. Our other sibling research project in Brisbane, Australia (Queensland University of Technology) carried out lab-based research measuring heart rate, eye-tracking, facial expressions and galvanic skin response of 69 children aged 7–13 in Australia playing digital games.

How can children's digital play support their wellbeing?

Our combined research shows that digital games, when designed well, can support children's subjective wellbeing across eight unique dimensions. These are presented in the RITEC Framework.

1. **Autonomy**. In a context where children in many formal learning settings are experiencing increasing pressure and reduced opportunities to engage in freer play, digital play experiences represent an important chance for children to experience control and autonomy.

2. **Competence**. Digital play can enable children to experience mastery and feel they can achieve. For example, gaining increasing skills and knowledge in relation to FIFA through continued practice contributed to an important sense of competence for nine year old Romeos in Cyprus.

3. **Emotions**. Allowing children to experience a range of emotions, be aware of their emotions and be able to regulate their emotions.

4. **Relationships**. Digital play allows children to experience connectedness with others, manage social connections, feel that they belong and be aware of others.

5. **Creativity**. Digital play allows children to be open to a range of experiences, imagine different possibilities, act on original ideas and make things. In Australia, 12 year old Ethan found that games like *Zelda* encouraged him to think critically and respond in his own, creative way to challenges.

6. **Identities**. Digital play allows children to explore, construct and express facets of themselves and others.

7. **Diversity, equity and inclusion**. Wellbeing in relation to diversity, equity and inclusion was supported when there was a good level of representation of diverse individuals within digital games played by children and when these games supported the full engagement of a diverse range of children, including those with different bodies, physical and learning disabilities and differences, different material circumstances and different deep interests, needs and desires.

8. **Safety and security**. Safety and security are of fundamental importance for digital design and have been extensively covered by a wide range of other studies. Wellbeing in terms of safety and security was supported when digital play experiences underpinned a sense of physical, emotional and economic safety.

Digital play design for wellbeing

The research not only sheds light on the influence of digital games on children's wellbeing but also provides valuable insights for those working in the children's media industry, including, but not limited to, game producers and designers. We are now working with partners to ensure these findings inform how the gaming experiences of tomorrow are designed for children. For example, to foster childrens' sense of autonomy, a game should offer opportunities for them to exercise control, make decisions about gameplay and develop their own strategies for progression. To nurture creativity, a game should facilitate free exploration and problem-solving, and support children to create their own characters or narratives. Design guidance relating to all eight dimensions of wellbeing can be found in our research report.

However, importantly, particular design features of digital games sometimes supported, or did not support, different aspects of wellbeing for different children. For example, being able to skip levels supported a sense of autonomy and competence for some children, but others felt skipping levels was a form of failure. Another example is that the choice of different ways to solve puzzles afforded autonomy for some children, whilst others felt the game did not offer opportunities to play in flexible ways.

Why does paying attention to difference matter?

In this sense, it is vital to understand that children and their families are diverse. Children's digital play choices and practices were influenced by diverse and often intersecting factors in our study. These included specific family dynamics, practices and cultures, neurodiversity, physical differences or disabilities, a range of emotional and learning needs and dynamics between different environments. Most compellingly, however, children's digital play choices and practices were associated with very different deep interests, desires and needs, understood in the present study as 'digital play drivers'. 11 drivers of children's digital play were important in different children's lives during the study. For example, some children's digital play was driven by a need to understand, care about and attend to the needs of other people, animals, communities and environments. Some children, such as six year old Anna in South Africa, engaged in digital play practices associated with empathy, nurture and tending for imagined others. Anna's wellbeing was particularly supported by digital games that allowed her to tend to others, such as through a hotel simulation game, where she helped her imaginary guests. Meanwhile, some children's digital play was driven by the need to understand, and meet, one's own emotional needs. For example, in the UK, ten year old Hailey's

©Alexandra Francis

explorations in the virtual worlds of *Pokémon* and *Zelda* were strongly motivated by a desire for escapism and emotional release, contrary to sometimes challenging social dynamics in other domains of her life. All 11 'digital play drivers' are discussed in detail in our research report.

In some cases, there are clear connections between digital play drivers and life experiences and factors. However, it is ultimately not possible to fully answer why children are driven by particular deep interests, desires and needs at different points in their lives. What is clear is that no single digital play experience can be all things to all children. By using the RITEC framework as a tool and considering the design recommendations provided in our research report, designers will increase the likelihood that their games contribute positively to children's wellbeing. A positive approach within this would be to design digital games with the particular needs of one or more groups of children in mind. It is clear that, in order for the digital play needs of all children to be supported, a diverse range of carefully designed games should proliferate.

Though work with designers and policymakers is ongoing, we are already excited by the potential of the RITEC child-centred wellbeing framework. The eight dimensions described in the framework aren't intended as hoops for the children's media industry to jump through; rather we hope they open up new possibilities for those whose digital products and services are used by children. The different dimensions offer opportunities for children's digital play designers in particular to imagine diverse possibilities for the future of children's play as they continue to innovate.

To learn more about the RITEC project, our family case study research and findings, and our recommendations for the children's media industry and policy makers, visit: https://sites.google.com/sheffield.ac.uk/digitalplayandwellbeing/. You can read the full research report from our family case study research at: https://sites.google.com/sheffield.ac.uk/digitalplayandwellbeing/all-publications.

Photo by Vitaly Gariev on Unsplash

Anonymous Apps: *Gossip Girl* For The Platform Generation

 **Dr Ysabel Gerrard**, Senior Lecturer in Digital Communication, University of Sheffield

Have you ever heard of the social media app Sarahah? No…? Ok, well what about Tellonym, LMK, CuriousCat, or Whisper? If your answer is still 'no', which it likely is, then don't worry – there are very good reasons for this, and I'm going to walk you through them.

The apps I've listed above fall under the 'anonymous app' genre. When you use a particular anonymous app, you know who you are sending a message to, but your recipient will not know that you are the person who sent it to them. Despite their namesake, anonymous apps don't actually enable true anonymity, as their users are technically traceable through things like their internet protocol (IP) address. Nonetheless, this is the name people use to describe the apps and, crucially, it's how people *feel* when they experience them. The apps typically work by connecting users to their already-existing networks on other social media apps, like Instagram or Snapchat, or to other app users who are physically located within a certain radius. This partly explains why apps like Yik Yak work so well within schools.

It's no exaggeration to say that anonymous apps are tremendously popular with children in many places around the world, and yet we know so little about them. Take Sarahah as an example: founded in 2016, Sarahah was initially designed to be used in Saudi Arabian corporate settings for employees to leave constructive feedback for their bosses. But the app was hijacked by teens from all around the world, at one point attracting a staggering 300 million users from over 30 countries, including Egypt, India, Japan, the UK and the US. Sarahah was repurposed by teens as a Q&A app, where a user could create an account, ask people a question, and then receive anonymised responses from just about anyone. When people call Sarahah an overnight success, they mean it: the app jumped from #104 to #1 in the Apple App Store charts in only three days. And Ask.fm – an anonymous website-turned-app, founded in 2010, whose users can ask questions either privately to individual users, or publicly via their profile – at one point handled 20,000 questions *per minute*.

Readers might therefore be wondering: if anonymous apps are even close to being as popular as I'm claiming, then why haven't more people heard of them? The answer to this question lies in the apps' failures.

Why do anonymous apps fail?

Individual anonymous apps usually fall victim to their own success. That is, a new app will become *popular by surprise*, rising to the top of app charts at breakneck speed, garnering millions of downloads and outpacing its mainstream rivals before being pulled for safety concerns, or being taken down by its own founder. Let's return to Sarahah here: although researchers don't know much about the kinds of questions teens asked on the app, we know respondents weren't always on their best behaviour. Anyone with or without a Sarahah account could reply to people's questions and so, naturally, the app was plagued with more complaints of bullying than its three (yes, three) staff members could safely handle. Quite predictably, Sarahah was removed from app stores in 2018.

Crucial for readers to note is that the above-described 'Sarahah saga' wasn't especially unique. An anonymous app called YOLO – an acronym for 'you only live once' – faced a similar fate. Launched in 2019, YOLO was an ephemeral social media anonymous Q&A app, that could be embedded into Snapchat: whose users could send images and videos to each other that will disappear within a certain timeframe. Rocketing to the top position in US app stores only a week after launching, YOLO users could request anonymised responses to a question from their Snapchat network. But as YOLO founder Gregoire Henrion has said:

> "It was not supposed to be a success. It was just for us to learn… Let's just put it on the App Store and see how people behave. It went 100% viral. It's crazy. Even we didn't believe our eyes when we saw that [it went to #1]."[1]

Following a US-based lawsuit filed in 2020 following the suicide of 16 year old Carson James Bride, Snap Inc announced it would prevent YOLO from integrating into Snapchat.

While bullying can take place on any social app, the argument goes that people are more likely to bully others when their identity is unknown. This is because of something called the *online disinhibition* effect: when people say and do things online "that they wouldn't ordinarily say and do in the face-to-face world. They loosen up, feel less restrained, and express themselves more openly".[2] But there's a real chicken-and-egg formulation to understanding bullying on anonymous apps: do the apps attract bullying behaviours because communication is anonymised, or do app users – exposed to bad press about the apps' dangers – behave badly because that's what they think the app is for?

Clearly, anonymous apps – which often become very popular, very quickly – are often not adequately staffed or technically designed to cope with bad behaviour, and so they are removed from app stores after a run of bad press, earning their rightful place in the social media Hall of Shame. The main reason anonymous apps fail is therefore not simply because they attract bullying behaviours: it's because their popularity outpaces their growth as app companies, meaning the safety mechanisms we're used to on more mainstream platforms simply aren't present. Anonymous apps are perceived to be (and

---

[1] Constine, 2019, #1 app YOLO Q&A is the Snapchat platform's 1st hit. TechCrunch. [Online]. Available at: https://techcrunch.com/2019/05/08/download-yolo-app/.
[2] Suler, J. 2004, The online disinhibition effect. CyberPsychology and Behavior. 7(3). p.321

sometimes genuinely are) dangerous for their young users because their meteoric rise to the top of app store charts makes them difficult to moderate, not because they enable anonymity.

Why are anonymous apps enduringly popular?

At this stage, readers are likely thinking: "anonymous apps sound awfully dangerous and probably haven't earned their place in the world." I'd be lying if I said I hadn't had the same thoughts. But with any communication technology, it's important to tell the stories of the good alongside the bad. In my forthcoming book with the University of California Press, I tell plenty of stories about English teens whose experiences with anonymous apps are simply *ok*, sometimes even fun. This is partly because the apps enable identity exploration. As Davis puts it:

> "...questions of identity – the sense of who one is and in what one believes – loom large for adolescents in Western societies. It is during this stage of development that individuals contemplate for the first time such questions as 'Who am I? How do I fit into the world around me?'"[3]

Anonymous app users don't have to put their names or faces to what they say, meaning their extreme popularity among adolescents makes perfect sense. Teens want to discuss certain topics on the apps – like bodily functions, compliments about personality or appearance, gender identity, homelife dynamics, mental health issues, and romantic relationships – because they are socially *stigmatised*, and can therefore be difficult to discuss with people they know.[4]

At this point, you might also be thinking "well, why should I care? Why do anonymous apps matter to me, in my field?" They should matter to us for many reasons, perhaps most obviously because they sometimes pose genuine dangers to children's safety. But anonymous apps also matter because, whether we like it or not, they form part of contemporary childhood, particularly adolescence, for many children around the world. They can be as much a part of childhood as the apps that spring straight to our minds when we hear the phrase 'social media', yet they continue to receive precious little public attention.

Photo by Luke Porter on Unsplash

---

[3] Davis, K. 2012, Friendship 2.0: adolescents' experiences of belonging and self-disclosure online. Journal of Adolescence. 35(6), p.1528.
[4] Goffman, E. 1963/1990. *Stigma: notes on the management of spoiled identity*. Harmondsworth: Penguin.

Social Media, Kidinfluencers And The Changing Discourse On Childhood

 **Dr Jane O'Connor**, Associate Professor of Childhood Studies, Birmingham City University

The proliferation of children becoming famous through social media channels such as YouTube/YouTube Kids, Instagram and TikTok surface important and difficult questions about the wellbeing of children, their relationship with public facing media and the boundaries of parent–child relationships.

Nearly one in three preteens list 'influencer' as a career goal,[1] perhaps unsurprising as child influencers can earn six figure incomes and appear to enjoy lives of unimaginable fun and privilege.

For example, Ryan Koji, star of *Ryan's World* on YouTube, has nearly 40 million subscribers and earns an estimated $30 million per year for producing content including toy reviews, prank videos and science experiments. Similarly, *Mila and Emma*, the 'sassiest twins on the internet', regularly share their five year old wisdom with 1.53 million subscribers on topics such as boyfriends, make-up and going to the gym.

However, health experts have warned of the profound risk of harm that social media presents to children, especially girls, due to the promotion of idealised, unattainable versions of beauty, constant comparison to peers and the focus on external signifiers of self-worth.[2] Unwelcome predatory followers are also a growing issue, with Meta recently disclosing that 500,000 child Instagram accounts had 'inappropriate' interactions every day.

As an expert on the cost of fame to adults who were former child stars in the more traditional mediums of cinema, TV and pop music, my concern for these child influencers is the potential long term impact of such early fame and public exposure.

Former child stars of stage and screen have often expressed sadness and anger about their atypical childhoods and the disruption to 'normal' parent–child relationships that their childhood fame involved. Parents as managers is rarely a comfortable setup. As children are not allowed to have their own Instagram account or create a YouTube channel until they are 13 it seems inevitable that contemporary child stars of social media are being enabled and facilitated by their parents who

---

[1] https://theharrispoll.com/briefs/lego-group-kicks-off-global-program-to-inspire-the-next-generation-of-space-explorers-as-nasa-celebrates-50-years-of-moon-landing/
[2] https://www.nytimes.com/2023/05/23/health/surgeon-general-social-media-mental-health.html

presumably also benefit from the financial aspects of their child's microcelebrity status.

Where does that leave the normalised social, cultural and legal boundaries around childhood that have protected children since Victorian times? These include the discourses that identify children as innocent and requiring adult protection, the laws around child labour and education, and the traditional caring and emotional relations between children and their parents whereby the child is financially dependent until they are 18. Transgressing these social boundaries, which have been constructed to maintain childhood as a protected space in which children can grow up shielded from the concerns and responsibilities of adulthood, is dangerous. When children have direct access to the world via public facing media they are vulnerable not only to inappropriate attention from strangers, but also to exploitation by the adults who are meant to be looking after them.

Can children really understand the long term consequences of early fame? Former child stars of the 1980s such as Macaulay Culkin and Drew Barrymore have expressed regret at being child stars and missing out on a 'normal' childhood. Many other child stars have experienced drug and alcohol addiction, broken marriages, mental health issues, even time in jail as they have struggled to cope with the impact of having reached the peak of their career as a child, frequently feeling like a failure as a teen and adult. Many talk about the shame when people say to them: "Didn't you used to be…?"

© Photo by Tim Gouw on Unsplash

It's hard to know how this will play out for today's crop of child influencers and social media stars. Maybe they are more resilient than former generations, more media savvy? Maybe the money they make now will insulate them from difficult times ahead when they may lose their followers if their face no longer fits or they run out of ideas for content. One thing is for sure, you can't go on being a cute kid forever and, if that is your pull and purpose online, it has a sell by date.

Emotional fallout aside, in terms of legislation to protect kidinfluencers there is a huge gap in current regulations in the UK. The House of Commons Culture, Media and Sport Committee published a report in 2022 recommending that the government 'urgently' addresses gaps in UK child labour and performance regulations that are leaving child influencers unprotected.[3] They recommended that new legislation should include provisions on working hours and conditions and protecting a child's earnings, stating:

> "We are deeply concerned that a lack of action in the booming influencer market will lead to even more children in the industry being exploited."

So far, no moves towards actioning such legislation have been made.

The ways in which child stars are created and treated in a society shows us what is valued about children in the wider culture. It is chilling to reflect on what the unchallenged rise of the image perfect, lucrative kidinfluencer may be telling us about our current ideals of childhood. Social media allows children to be valued on looks, charm and financial viability and, if social media continues to be broadly unregulated, a generation may well grow up with the message that this is all that matters.

---

[3] https://committees.parliament.uk/work/1126/influencer-culture/news/170678/influencer-culture-mps-call-for-action-on-advertising-and-employment-rules-to-protect-children-and-online-performers/

Cosmic Kids Yoga: From **Birthday Parties To Apps** And Beyond!

 **Jaime Amor**, Founder, *Cosmic Kids Yoga*

Hello! I'm Jaime. I've been making *Cosmic Kids Yoga* with my husband Martin for 12 years. I'll share what's worked for us as we've developed original content, tried to run our business in an efficient way and worked hard to build an honest brand. Perhaps you're curious to know what our experience has been. I hope that sharing what's happened to us over these years will help you.

Cosmic Kids Yoga really began as a tool. It served a very clear purpose for me – to hold kids' attention at birthday parties. Necessity is the mother of invention! Yoga was in my life already – I'd been introduced to it as a teenager by my mum, and later, by my voice teacher at drama school. Then as a jobbing actor, making ends meet at the weekend entertaining at kids' parties, I found a new use for it.

As a kids' party entertainer, your job is to keep 25 or so four to seven year olds entertained for two hours. I realised pretty quickly that getting their attention in the first 20 minutes was critical to my success. So I came up with a plan. I would tell the kids:

> "Try not to worry but – any minute now – a WITCH WILL BE ARRIVING AT THE PARTY. She is coming to steal your birthday powers! (This is jeopardy when you're five.) The good news is you can stop the witch with these five special moves (all yoga poses). If we do the moves when she challenges us, she will simply melt into a puddle on the floor and we will save the day."

I had their attention! Then I'd teach the five magic moves – Witch's Cat, Cauldrons, Witch's Party, Witch's Fire and Broomsticks!

All of a sudden, there was a chill in the air, a strange smell... "Can you smell it? The witch is HERE." I started to have a funny turn, becoming possessed by the witch – one eye closing, wiggly crooked fingers, my voice all cackly and witchy. Now in full witch mode (though still dressed as a fairy) I challenged the children: "you can't possibly know the special moves that would stop me taking all your birthday powers!" Of course, all would rise up heroically and demonstrate that they bloomin' well did! Off they went – with me (as the witch) challenging them with each move... and each time they executed, I weakened and faltered – with the final move causing me to emit a large raspberry sound as I crumpled to the floor. The children are jubilant! They did it. Their special moves were the source of their power. And I woke up as the fairy again to share in the joy.

I decided to train as an adult yoga teacher. During my training I kept seeing how it could be adapted for kids and used as a language to tell stories – yoga adventures. The kids could be heroes as they did the moves. I became interested in the ethos of yoga, and realised I could land simple messages for a happy life, and introduce tools to genuinely help kids become resilient. I wished I'd had this when I was six!

I approached schools and nurseries, and hired village halls and community centres to get my classes going. Not everyone got it, but eventually I convinced one school to go for it.

By late 2011, 18 months since I'd started my classes, I was busy – teaching 15 classes a week. At that point, my husband went to Silicon Valley on a study tour with corporate folk from the UK to meet various tech companies in California – YouTube, Google, Cisco, Apple. Broadband was taking off so video was becoming a big focus for all of those companies. Martin called me from San Francisco to share this – and suggested we could try and do something with video. Neither of us had really used a camera before, but video would allow us to reach a lot more kids and they could do their yoga anytime. I'd been heaving my big bag of yoga mats to school after school with 15 kids paying £4.50 a session – it was time to try this.

We thought it would be cool to make the yoga stories playful and immersive. Using a green screen, we could cut me out and put me in a cartoon world. I got a pink onesie – the same as One Direction were wearing in their 2012 live tour – so I'd look comfortable, approachable and a little bit down with the kids!

A camera operator friend of ours met us at our local sports and social club, armed with a big green curtain. We shot three yoga adventures that day, ones that I'd been doing in my classes. I did them as if the camera was the kid, looking straight down the lens, which has ended up being one of the most powerful engagement tools we know.

Martin figured out how greenscreen keying worked, then we hesitated. We wondered if it was a bit weird. A bit silly. We sat on the three videos for a couple of months.

Finally, in May 2012, we put our heads above the parapet. We set up a YouTube channel, uploaded the first video and hit the publish button!

First, I shared it with all the kids in my regular classes. They liked it! And they liked being able

© Cosmic Kids Yoga

to do their yoga when they wanted. They regarded YouTube as a super cool place full of fun things. Their parents approved because it was better for them than most of the other stuff on there.

It wasn't long before the global teaching community found us. Teachers are the most eagle-eyed resource hunters on the planet! *Cosmic Kids Yoga* on YouTube was picked up as a free tool to manage the energy of kids in their classrooms, involving them in movement and story. It worked the same way as it had at the parties, with the added benefit of creating calmer more focused behaviours in the classroom.

Our mantra has always been that if the kids love it, it'll do well. That has underpinned everything we've made. As we started our channel, our goal was to bring yoga to as many kids as possible, in a way that works for them. There is something so honest and transparent about how you iterate your content on YouTube – you steadily grow and improve, and you take your audience with you on that journey. They see it all and contribute directly to it, because you are in contact with them, taking on new ideas for what else they'd like to see in your content. It is such a great organic way to make content that folks want.

In 2015 teachers started asking us to create an app. Many school internet firewalls were blocking YouTube and we'd had reports from teachers about inappropriate ads before our videos. A 35 year old in Denver may be an appropriate target for *Paranormal Activity 3* trailers, but this wasn't so good for a classroom full of five year olds. Vimeo had recently launched a white label video app platform, so we took the plunge and invested in it, hoping we could grow paying subscribers. It served a tiny proportion of our audience and initially we weren't sure it was going to take off.

Ultimately, it was a good decision. In September 2019, YouTube settled out of court for 170 million US dollars with the US Federal Trade Commission for breaching privacy regulations. In January 2020 new rules at YouTube kicked in and our YouTube revenue dropped by 90%. If we were to continue, we needed our app to succeed and for folks to subscribe to it, to fund making the videos.

Then on March 23rd 2020 lockdown began and we were told to stay at home. Teachers sent students home with a list of resources to help parents with homeschooling, and – globally – *Cosmic Kids* was on many of those lists. Our views went from a healthy 100,000 a day to one million a day. The phone started ringing as journalists all over the world wanted to profile me. Kids everywhere were suddenly doing *Cosmic Kids Yoga* videos. Kim Kardashian's daughter, North, appeared in the background of a make-up vlog trying to decide which *Cosmic Kids* video to do. Barack Obama tweeted an image of a little girl doing *Cosmic Kids* with a comment about the pressures of homeschooling on parents. Happily we had eight years' worth of videos on YouTube and a whole load of fresh new videos on our app so there was lots to keep everyone busy.

Partners started getting in touch, wanting us to make yoga adventures based on their properties. We worked with Paramount on a *Sonic the Hedgehog* yoga adventure; Procter and Gamble on a brand of soap for handwashing; Fox with a new *Masked Singer* series; Hasbro/E One and *My Little Pony*; Sir Paul McCartney wanted a yoga adventure based on his *Grandude* kids book; even the European Space Agency wanted me to create a yoga plan for their astronaut to do in space.

After eight years of very steady growth, a little hockey stick shape happened in our analytics. We were a household name among parents of primary school-aged kids. Things have calmed down a little now. Kids are back at school so we get one view for the whole classroom rather than 20 in their homes – but we're glad that those 20–25 kids in the classroom are all watching and doing yoga. That was our goal all along.

Just prior to the pandemic, we'd had a call from Ian France, a commissioning editor at Sky Kids to tell us how much his children loved *Cosmic Kids*, asking us whether we'd be interested in making a show for Sky. At the time we didn't have an idea so said maybe one day.

Then last year, we heard again from Ian – and this time gave it some proper thought. We had an idea and both Ian and Lucy Murphy, Director of Kids Content, were keen on it. We're on a new learning curve as we make *Cosmic Kids* work for TV. We are working alongside incredibly talented TV folk at Banijay / Zodiak Kids and, with Ian and Lucy guiding us, we are taking the best of what we've learnt so far and blending that with all the production clout of TV. It feels like a natural next step.

Meanwhile, we just shot our 100th yoga adventure. Somebody once said, "find what you love doing, enjoy doing it and then do it for other people". We feel privileged that we have found this in kids' yoga and look forward to the future of *Cosmic Kids*.

Sport Will Save Us

Maurice Wheeler, CEO, We are Family

In December 2022, nearly 90,000 spectators packed into the airy dome of Qatar's Lusail stadium for the FIFA World Cup Final. After a grisly match and a grislier overtime, Argentina squeezed out a dramatic victory over France in a white-knuckled penalty shootout. The crowd went wild.

The frenzied spectators at the stadium were just the tip of the iceberg, viewership-wise. When all was said and done, some 1.5 billion people watched the final. Nearly 5 billion tuned in to some part of the 2022 World Cup. That's more than half of all the humans alive today – and it's not hard to see why they wanted to watch.

Far more than a sum of its parts, football, and sport generally, is a very effective vehicle for storytelling. It gives us heroes and underdogs to root for, shows us what it's like to overcome struggles, and surprises us with endings we don't always expect.

These are just some of the reasons that sport is the backbone of so much entertainment. From live events like the World Cup, to sport documentaries like the recent Netflix Formula 1 smash *Drive to Survive*, to comedy dramas like *Ted Lasso* or 'reality' shows like the BBC's recent *Gladiators* revival; sports content is huge in the adult world.

While there is some popular kids sports content, from dramas like *Jamie Johnson* and *Mustangs FC* to the TikTok videos that football clubs and players produce, it definitely feels like much more could be happening.

We are Family recently carried out research with over 4,300 children worldwide (1,000 in the UK) aiming to better understand which sports kids are watching and playing, how often, and what stops them from getting into a sport or continuing with it. When we spoke to kids we learned that over 65% of 7–12 year olds in the UK consider themselves sports fans. The number one way they like to indulge in their fandom? Consuming sports content.

It's an interesting pressure point in a fast changing media landscape. The latest 'gilded age of television' is coming to an end as subscription video on demand (SVOD) services begin to seek profit over growth and public broadcasters continue to get squeezed. Today's kids are largely in control of their own devices, too, so parents and broadcasters no longer control viewing the way they once did. YouTube (and TikTok, to some extent), with their unending content supplies, seem like they're going to continue their reign as kids' media kingpins for the next few years at least.

For *any* content to succeed now, it needs to be highly financially viable, which means internationally sellable, evergreen and cheap to produce. For the most part, kids' media has adapted to tick these boxes, but these are tough times for kids content and the whole industry has seen a decline in revenues and therefore content production. So can sports content fill the gaps?

Maybe. While the potential audiences are there (as the World Cups' viewership shows: half of humanity is nothing to sniff at), generally speaking, sports content is not very evergreen, is pricey to make (and get the rights to), and doesn't always translate internationally. That's not to say there aren't opportunities but to appeal to kids and be financially viable, both media and sports organisations have to shift from the current status quo.

Insights and opportunities

Put all the content on all the channels

85% of tween fans check social media for sports updates and highlights weekly, with 23% doing so daily. On average, tweens use 4.7 different platforms each week to watch sports content, and nearly 60% prefer content from official pages versus 40% from fan accounts. As tweens get older, they also start looking for digital communities of like-minded fans; one in five 11–12 year olds say that they rely on online platforms like Reddit and Discord for sports news.

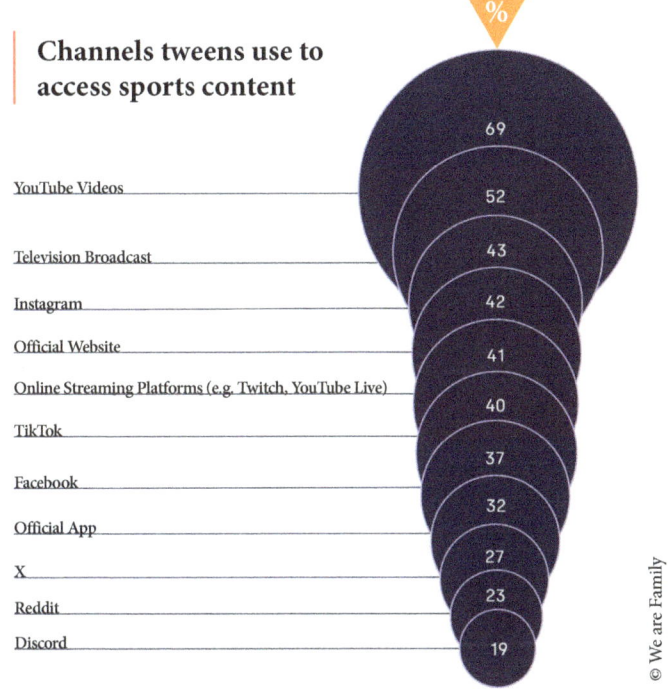

Channels tweens use to access sports content (%)

Channel	%
YouTube Videos	69
Television Broadcast	52
Instagram	43
Official Website	42
Online Streaming Platforms (e.g. Twitch, YouTube Live)	41
TikTok	40
Facebook	37
Official App	32
X	27
Reddit	23
Discord	19

© We are Family

This means today's tweens consume a *lot* of different types of sports content across a lot of channels. Each of these channels or platforms and engagements scratch a different itch, whether it's getting to know their favourite players, laughing at bloopers, or just watching a team's crazy sporting prowess. To make the most of these multichannel engagement patterns, companies should package their sports content in a variety of formats, including slick 'official' content and user-generated content.

Recalibrate the value of live sports

While nearly half (42%) of tweens still regularly tune into live broadcasts, this traditional form of watching sports is (unsurprisingly) losing its dominant influence. The reduction in live TV consumption is an industry-wide phenomenon, driven by the general fragmentation of media, the increased competition from other platforms, and changing content format preferences.

Given the popularity of TikTok and YouTube, it's not particularly surprising that tweens prefer watching short clips and compilations over long-form content. What's more unexpected is that these algorithm-driven platforms are making it less important for sports content to be 'new' to capture attention. Kids are just as open to watching older sports clips on these platforms, as evidenced by the swathes of Lionel Messi fan accounts creating snappy, viral TikTok edits of his best highlights over the last decade.

Sporting rights owners need to think about how they can reengineer their business models if this 'golden asset' continues to lose appeal with kids and teens.

Treat sport as entertainment

This is not new at all, but in our research it was clear that tweens were looking for all the surrounding content and not just what happens in the actual sporting event. With Netflix willing to pay $5B for the rights to air WWE for the next ten years, and to pay an alleged $40M for the Jake Paul and Mike Tyson fight, it's clear that the stories and content surrounding the event is just as, if not more important, than the event itself.

In our research, we found that players like Messi become the protagonists of the team's (and their own) stories. Generally, tweens like characters that are relatable and aspirational. So, a tween's favourite sports star tends to play the same sport as the child (making them relatable) and are admired for their skills and achievements (aspirational).

Broaden the definition of sports

39% of tweens think that eSports should be defined as a sport, 10% have participated in an eSports tournament and 31% have watched a live eSports stream. While eSports has been an 'up and coming' category for a few years now it is still building momentum and has proven it is not a flash in the pan. Today's tweens are definitely more open minded on what constitutes 'sport' than their parents are.

Think And Wonder, Wonder And Think: Children And Philosophy

 **Sally Latham**, Philosophy Lecturer and Media Education Consultant

Children are natural philosophers. Although we have all experienced the never-ending 'why?' when we make 'unreasonable' requests of children, such as that they put on their coat, so many of the questions that children ask are genuinely philosophical. This article argues firstly that nurturing philosophy in children is of primary importance and, secondly, that children's media has a vital role to play in this process.

Encouraging philosophical thought and critical thinking in children is important for many reasons. 'Philosophy' has grand, elitist connotations, but the word comes from the Greek literally meaning *love (philo) of wisdom (sophia)*. If there is one thing children like, it's to know things. When children ask "can dogs be sad? Why doesn't my sister like jelly when it's so yummy? Why do grown-ups get to do things I can't? Why should I be kind to animals?" they are doing philosophy. The first thing that we as adults must do is to validate their inquiries so that children feel that their questions are important. Without an outlet for philosophical thoughts we run into the danger of treating their questions as an annoyance or trivial, of making children think they are not worth asking.

The idea of bringing philosophy into the education system has been around for a while. SAPERE (the Society for the Advancement of Philosophical Enquiry and Reflection in Education) is the UK's national charity for Philosophy for Children (P4C) and has had a huge impact in bringing philosophy to schools and in training teachers to deliver philosophy in the classroom. There have been numerous studies showing the positive impact of P4C on cognitive ability, mental health and wellbeing, social skills and resistance to extremism. A report by the Education Endowment Foundation found the impact to be the greatest on disadvantaged pupils.[1]

We are being told we live in a VUCA world, one of volatility, uncertainty, complexity and ambiguity. We know that we need to educate children to think critically in a world of fake news and political rhetoric. We know that children are exposed to a minefield of unregulated media content, and if we don't equip them to question what they are told then we leave them vulnerable to misinformation. But if we expect them to be thinking critically when scrolling their phones at 15, we need to start nurturing their reasoning skills and questions as soon as they start asking

---

[1] https://educationendowmentfoundation.org.uk/projects-and-evaluation/projects/philosophy-for-children

them at age three. To be clear, this doesn't mean giving them the answers, it means validating the questions. There could and should be a number of different answers to consider to any philosophical question, which in itself is something important for children to learn. We need to equip children with the means to understand, cope with and shape this VUCA world, and to do so we have to move beyond the confines of the National Curriculum in which success is measured in exam results – and teach children to really think.

Labour has already pledged to embed oracy in the English education system, with the ethos that children are given new opportunities by being able to express themselves clearly and confidently. Philosophical questioning and debate will have an important contribution to this. As Stephen Coleman, Professor of Political Policy at the University of Leeds points out, this isn't about using fancy words and taking elocution lessons, but rather confidence and self-expression. He goes on to say "voice is a very, very important tool particularly for the most disadvantaged young people in society."[2] If children can't articulate their ideas, and defend them rigorously, then their ideas won't be heard as they grow and navigate a world of loud voices.

There is already quite rightly a momentum to highlight the importance of play for early development. For example the government's 2019 'Chat, Play and Read' home learning environment campaign encouraged parents to communicate, read and play with their children before school age.[3] Philosophical thinking is just as important to a child's development as play, although the two are also intertwined. Nancy Richards, writing in Paul Lindley's *Raising the Nation* (2023), highlights the importance of play in developing the concept and principles of democracy. She argues that through free play children learn self-governance, emotional regulation, how to develop rules, collaboration and cooperation. Yet 'hypervigilant parenting' and 'overscheduled kids' mean that free play is declining, along with the art of democracy. By controlling our children we negate their ability to work out social problems for themselves. The same is true for free thinking as it is for free play. Unless we give children the chance to think, to find their own consistencies and recognise their own inconsistencies, we do them a disservice by not equipping them to navigate a world of uncertainty, dubious influence and untruth. Unfortunately we are often so concerned with a results-based education that we don't have time for unquantifiable free thought.

As I have said, philosophy is being introduced into schools with success. But it should not be confined to schools, and this is where children's media has a crucial role to play. Sophie Giblan, also writing in *Raising the Nation*, proposes the idea of a more developed 'National Play at Home Scheme', providing parents with the tools and instructions on how to play effectively with their children. I propose that we should have a similar scheme for 'Think at Home', where we equip parents to encourage philosophical and critical

---

[2] https://www.theguardian.com/education/2023/jul/07/labour-oracy-plan-children-speaking-skills-england-schools?CMP=share_btn_url

[3] https://literacytrust.org.uk/news/chat-play-read-campaign-announced-encourage-learning-home/

discussion with their children. Media is crucial for this process as it brings philosophy into the home. There is, of course, educational children's media that is hugely entertaining whilst still providing them with factual knowledge. But what is missing is the media that encourages children to go away and ask questions, critically evaluate the world around them and have philosophical conversations. One sign of a good children's TV show is that it affects a child's life beyond the seven minutes or so of entertainment, to impact on a child's life once the screen is off. At the moment, many shows can do this through play, if they are treated as springboards for imagination. I've been on a few *Andy's Dinosaur Adventures* myself. But where are the shows that are genuinely entertaining, with characters that children engage with and storylines that excite them, yet at the same time also encourage children to go away and *ask questions*? This should be something that is happening from preschool upwards and is the motivation behind Adastra Development's *Wilma Wonderwig*, a preschool show currently in development, that presents a cast of funny, warm and zany characters that children will relate to and grow to love, but that also provokes philosophical thought. Children will enjoy the stories but also go away and have their own 'wonder moments' about their own lives and experiences. Such programs should be made as accessible as possible to allow children to develop their voice, assess the world around them and feel that their questions are valuable. This is a basic right of every child, just as much as learning to read and write. Programs such as *Sesame Street* knew the importance of bringing literacy and numeracy to disadvantaged children, but now we should be producing quality children's content, from preschool to teen audiences, that make sure children continue to think philosophically. It is important that this content is available to children from even the most disadvantaged backgrounds, for these are the children that need to have their voice heard the most. Every child starts as a philosopher, and it is our duty to make sure they continue to be one.

> "Think and wonder. Wonder and think."
> – Dr Seuss

> "For this feeling of wonder shows that you are a philosopher, since wonder is the only beginning of philosophy." – Plato

Image by rawpixel.com on Freepik

 **PLANT**

CONTENT FOR CHILDREN
WITH CHILDREN
BY CHILDREN

CYNNWYS
Ceidiog
CONTENT

CONNECTING BRANDS
WITH KIDS AND FAMILIES

SINCE 1999

RESEARCH
Full service agency and Kids Trends data

METAVERSE
We create award winning Roblox and Fortnite experiences

APPS & EDTECH
Our games are played by millions of kids and families

Dubit.io   research.dubit.io   hello@dubit.io

Playful Storytelling To Inspire Oracy

Lucy Walters, Storyteller, Actor and Presenter

"Wind your fishing rod and cast your line!" It's a Saturday morning in March and I'm at the British Library with a room full of children fishing words and sounds from a stream. "Gurgling, burbling, babbling, rippling!" we all say together. As the words are spoken and our fishing rods playfully bob *up and down*, a sound is played – the sound of a stream I recorded a few weeks earlier.

Another Saturday morning, but this time I'm on my hands and knees crouched down with a microphone next to a fast-flowing stream. It has rained a lot so the sounds of the water splish splash beautifully along. As is often the case, a dog walker passes by and shoots me a confused glance. "I'm a children's storyteller…," I say, "collecting sounds… for a new show." He politely nods and carries on.

My love of creating and telling playful stories is firmly rooted in the hours, days spent exploring outside as a child finding things to do, the stories I was read and told, and the children's television programmes I loved to watch. Children's television had a huge impact on me: the characters; the sets; the songs; how all this wonderful storytelling would spark ideas for creating my own stories, not to mention the clubs, badges, secret meetings, and all sorts of other ideas that would spin out of them. I recently sat down to watch an episode of *Play School* from 1979. And there it was. An episode on sounds! The brilliant Derek Griffiths pretends to play the xylophone after a masterclass from the percussionist, James Blades – at one point a homemade xylophone was used, made of long sticks and short sticks. As the music rang out in the studio, Derek would listen and imagine the correct instrument to act out and play. The children were encouraged to join in at home. The mixture of fun, games, song and live presenters blend beautifully to create imaginative, sparky storytelling. 45 years later, at my live storytelling event, children are joyfully playing, saying, seeing, imagining stories acted out through sounds, words, and actions.

Playful storytelling is not just for entertainment, it's a powerful tool for oracy at a time when 1.9 million children currently struggle with talking and understanding words.[1] By helping children to become effective speakers and listeners we help them to better understand themselves, each other and the world around them, in turn, supporting education attainment, wellbeing and social mobility. Live storytelling is wonderful; I love encouraging children to "join in with me" as we play with words and sounds, exploring rhythmic tones of language and voice. This approach combined with the broad reach of children's media, combining clever animation with live action, has the potential to create wide reaching change, embedding the joy of language, words and creativity.

---

[1] www.speechandlanguage.org.uk

I'm currently mid-way through a five-show theatre run of my new preschool storytelling show, *Lucy's Let's Tell a Story*, supporting language development, communication and play; the show inspired, in part, by the charming, lyrical storytelling of *Bagpuss*, when "Once upon a time, not so long ago, Emily found a thing." At the start of each show, I open my toy box to find simple objects sending us off on a story adventure. The show combines homemade props, animations from clipped together illustrations and playful songs to demonstrate how a story can be told in many different forms. And through these many different forms we make, sing, play and say our way through a story. By the end, the parents and especially grandparents are fully into it too!

My aim with playful storytelling has always been to help children find their voice. I'm excited about how children's media, woven richly in the fabric of our society, can work to inspire children's oracy. The one in five children struggling with talking and understanding words is the highest number with speech and language challenges ever recorded. Whatever form it may take, the twanking of the harp, the rustling reeds, the buzzing bees and the booming of the big bass drum are needed now more than ever.

Lucy's Let's Tell a Story Live

For The Love Of Play! From Ragdoll To *Mixmups*

Karen Newell, Play Consultant

Karen shares how understanding play theory and observing the responses of children has shaped her career from Ragdoll's **Teletubbies** *to* **Mixmups**, *a playful new preschool show on Milkshake!*

Play, to children, is like water and air: they need it to thrive, learn and grow. Understanding play theory and how it underpins everything little viewers do can help producers of preschool content connect with their audience on new levels.

I started my career as a play worker back in the 1990s, employed by local authority play services in London and Warwickshire. Working directly with children, knee-deep in sandpits, face paint and toys, I began a lifelong interest in observing the way that children play and how that can inform us as grownups to understand them and their worldview better.

In the late 90s I moved from grassroots play work to Ragdoll Productions as a children's responses researcher. I joined the company just as *Teletubbies* was becoming a preschooler phenomenon.

On my first day, I walked in to find myself right in the middle of the magical Teletubbies' house, a playful wonderland built by Anne Wood and Andrew Davenport, with a true appreciation of how to capture the wonder and curiosity of children and bring it to life with rolling green hills, bright colours and hopping rabbits!

Anne and Andrew were passionate about listening to the voices and responses of their viewers; they wanted to climb inside the minds of an audience, who, until this point, had been largely overlooked, very young children. They understood that the language of young children is play. Ragdoll valued children as independent thinkers and wanted to work with them in order to create more meaningful TV viewing experiences. The company was much more than just a production company, it was a child-centred research centre. It was my job to observe and gather audience responses to help Anne, Andrew and their creative team develop world-leading programming that engaged young children on their level.

To better connect with the audience and their worldview, Anne and Andrew taught me about play theory and play schemas, a set of play patterns that children use to explore and make sense of the world around them. Some children love to play with toy cars and enjoy the rotation of wheels, others like to wrap themselves in fabric and enjoy the sensation of envelopment. There is physical play, hanging upside down and exploring physics with your body, and transformative play, dressing up or combining things to make something new.

I spent hours watching footage of children watching Ragdoll shows in various forms of completion, like a kind of baby *Gogglebox*! I would observe their emotional responses to the screen. When do they smile? When do they laugh? When does their attention wander? When do they talk back to the TV and what do they say? When do they look to a companion to communicate about what they see on screen? When do they get up and run or shout "Again, again!" And when do they disengage?

I took a silent cut of a show that was in development to a school to observe how the children filled in the lack of dialogue and sound themselves. As a class of reception children watched in silence, they began to vocalise the action and encourage the characters to act in specific ways. "Quick, quick," "He's getting away," "Over there!" they shouted at the screen in response to the action. These children and their innate responses were helping us as producers to time and pace the subsequent narration of the show.

After ten years at Ragdoll, I left to have my own children and whilst working freelance and raising two children (one of whom is sight impaired) I began working with the writer and Executive Producer Rebecca Atkinson, who herself has hearing loss and is partially sighted. First, we launched the *Toy Like Me* campaign in 2015 to call on the global toy industry to better represent 150 million disabled children worldwide, and then later, when Rebecca began developing a new preschool brand for Channel 5 that we now know as *Mixmups* (produced by Mackinnon and Saunders and distributed by Raydar Media), I came on board to advise her as a play consultant for the show.

Mixmups

Rebecca wanted to build a brand around the magic of play and imagination and was keen to learn about how play theory and an understanding of play schemas could help her to create a world and characters which would connect with a young audience through their innate desire to play.

We began to observe children, and gather their views, only this time we were looking not just at how non-disabled children play, but also how disabled children play too. We engaged a group of junior consultants, listened to their voices over a number of years, and looked at how all children have different play personalities – we have all known that physical child who loves to throw themselves around, or the child who loves to create and make and stick and paint. We studied Stuart Brown, a leading academic in the field of play theory and his classification of play personalities.[1] He describes play character types, which Rebecca worked into the characters of Giggle, Pockets and Spin to give them relatable play personalities. Spin, the boisterous loud physical player, Giggle the exuberant creative player and Pockets, the gentle ordered introvert player.

© Mackinnnon and Saunders

Mixmups

Everything about *Mixmups* is powered by a deep understanding of play. Rebecca wove play schemas into every aspect of *Mixmups*' design, from the characters' appearance to the trio's Helter-Skelter home and garden in Mixington Valley. The show's Magic Mixing Box was designed as a toyetic transportation Tardis that takes in rotational play, containment play, transformative play and envelopment in one simple but glorious object of playful imagination. The magical transformation sequence in the show is activated by a humble wooden spoon – not just the brand's emblem, but a spoon is an object of playful significance, it is a child's first tool of independence, a rotational play item and something everyone can find at home to join in – we all know how children love to combine and mix to create something new, whether it's paint, cake mix or in the case of the *Mixmups*, magic sparkles!

It has been an honour, and above all, so much fun, to be able to carry all that I have learnt about play and play theory across my career into to help create *Mixmups* as a play brand for the new generation. In many ways, I feel *Mixmups* is a show that stands on the shoulders of Ragdoll's trailblazing legacy, which I was so lucky to be part of and learn from.

---

[1] https://nifplay.org/what-is-play/play-personalities/

Something Old, Something New: First Forays Into Children's TV

Chitra Soundar, Creator, Writer and Executive Producer

"Something old, something new, something borrowed, something due." No, I'm not talking about getting married. I never talk about getting married, one of the many ways I disappointed my parents. I'm actually talking about my foray into children's TV and what I'm doing to stay in it.

Something old

I'm old, or should I say older than an average entrant into a new industry. I have switched careers four times now and each time I'm a bit older. I started my career as a tech educator a long time ago in India, moved into software development and then moved into corporate programme management, a fancy way to say I was very good at getting things done, large scale! Through all of this across two decades, I've also been writing children's books. Then a few years ago, I hung-up my GANTT charts and swapped them for cuddly toys to tell stories and write stories for three to ten year olds as a full-time job. This was my third career-switch and this time I could afford to stay at home and write books all my life. But there was one more unfulfilled dream yet to be realised – creating and writing for television and film.

Growing up in India, inside the studio town of Kollywood, I wrote plays and puppet shows, acted in my mum's improv plays, rubbing shoulders with our movie star neighbours, bumping into lyricists and composers, and accidentally walking into film shoots in the middle of our streets. I even managed to get a part as a backup dancer in a movie when I was 11. So, the need to see my scripts on TV and in movie form (possibly with some songs thrown in) was too big to ignore. I set about researching how to write for TV and where my interests lie.

Something new

Writing TV was something new. While I persisted trying to overcome the strange way of typing a story into Final Draft, I also wanted to better understand the industry and the craft. That's when my random subscription to the Children's Media Conference (CMC) newsletter brought me to a one-day industry event run on the eve of Manimation 2019. This was my first foray into understanding the UK kids' TV space. It was exhilarating to be able to talk to commissioners and production companies. I also met folks and exchanged my bookmarks for their visiting cards. Through those chats, I realised I already had a stepping stone – my books. I have already created characters and worlds. I know these characters and worlds intimately and I know which of them can work as TV. That something new – the foray into TV – was going to come from something old – my existing skills of writing books honed over 20 years.

And then of course the world shutdown and turned into…

INT: In the house – all the time. When life gives you lockdown, turn it into bootcamp – that's what I did. I spent the rest of the year writing treatments and scripts based on published and unpublished stories. I read craft books. I listened to writing and industry podcasts and I attended my first CMC – online! I listened to experts, noted down names, emailed people, connected via LinkedIn. And one of those people I connected with was Lotte Elwell at King Banana. I wrote to her asking for writing opportunities and what happened next was something out of a dream.

Something borrowed

A year before all this hoo-hah, I was working on a book series called *Nikhil and Jay*, inspired by my nephews who are of dual-heritage. They started saying and doing things that fascinated me. Having a children's author as an aunt is a blessing and a curse. They had access to lots of books, often signed for them, also curated for them. But the aunt was also constantly writing down ideas for stories from their shenanigans. We were a family who were close with both sides of the culture and I realised this was not reflected in the books that my nephews were reading.

Otter-Barry Books, founded by Janetta Otter-Barry, was keen to publish a series of books aimed at emerging readers, set in the UK and the *Nikhil and Jay* series was born! The first story in the book *Me Do It* was directly a quote from one of my nephews. Stories about eating mangoes the Indian way, celebrating star birthdays and having grandparents over from India were all rooted in reality, but fictionalised. These stories were episodic in nature and by this time, with my interest in TV getting stronger, I retained TV rights.

I strongly believed that this series needed to be made because we haven't seen South Asian children in lead roles on UK preschool television for decades. The stories were already beautifully British – a family with dual heritage, grandparents on both sides and two boys who are a great team together. And who better than the BBC to pitch it to? I pitched it to Michael Towner who was then acting as the children's commissioning exec for preschool, before Kate Morton had joined. At the same time, I also pitched this to King Banana who had read the stories still on the verge of publishing and things moved quickly from there.

This was July 2021 and you know what that meant – CMC of course! Again online! But there was one difference – I was not just a passive listener – I was pitching at the 'Put Your Money Where Your Mouth Is' session – I had submitted another idea to the competition and I was one of the finalists. My current agent Annette van Duren was able to check out my skills in real time before she signed me on.

Something due

It was not just Asian representation on screen that was overdue. I think it was more than that. Having entered a new industry, with the support of an agent who was opening doors, I have started writing on a few other shows while waiting for my show to be brought to life. As I navigated the world of pitching new shows, or looking for job opportunities, I often looked for others like me – from under-represented backgrounds wanting to do similar things. But there wasn't anything formal that was already out there.

I reached out to Greg Childs and asked if I could set something up at CMC to bring together people of colour working in kids' TV, games and film. And I joined hands with Nandita Jain, an animation director who I had connected with and is now a close friend. We set up our first two meetings at CMC 2023. We had over 40 people turn up and we set up Colourful Connections in Children's Media, UK (www.c3muk.com) and we have been meeting online since September 2023 – running masterclasses, offering each other support to ask questions and find a community.

While I was definitely NOT asked to write a testimonial for CMC, it might seem to you that way when reading this. But to be honest, if there was one thing that could track my progress from 2019 to today, that has been my involvement with the CMC. First in the one-day event, then at the online conference, then as a participant, then as a producer for events and being part of the Inclusivity committee. Through my participation and volunteering, I've networked with wonderful producers, writers, commissioners and more. I have learnt a lot listening to experts talk on stage and behind the scenes. And I've grown. My hope is that I can help others navigate their entry into this industry just as CMC did for me.

Some takeaways from my journey

Something old: Do the grunt work – practice your craft, don't give up and be prepared for luck.

Something new: Read up and research the industry – it's important to know the big picture and be a part of it.

Something borrowed: Network and ask for help – people are willing to help and support if they see your genuine passion. Don't be scared to shake hands, or connect online.

Image by pch.vector on Freepik

Something due: Volunteer in areas you want to be involved in. Or share your knowledge with someone, do a skill swap. Giving as well as taking will make the journey more fruitful even if the destination seems far away.

DARRALL MACQUEEN

Proud Sponsors of

THE CHILDREN'S MEDIA CONFERENCE
9-10-11 JULY 2024

Animation UK: the voice of the industry

Celebrating recent Tax Relief increases, we remain focused with a bold manifesto and a blueprint for sector growth. Read it here.

Amplify our impact and join our dynamic community. Discover exclusive member benefits, engage with innovative initiatives, and lend your voice to our campaigns at animationuk.org

To learn more about membership, please contact our Membership Manager ruxandra@ukscreenalliance.co.uk

ANIMATION UK

Remembering Ursula Von Zallinger

1939–2024

Ursula von Zallinger – Uli to her wide network of friends – first brought the world to PRIX JEUNESSE, to debate and honor excellence in children's television. Then, having listened to the global village that came to the Munich festival, she took PRIX JEUNESSE to the world.

The international children's television festival was initially dominated by European, Nordic and American public broadcasters. Uli, however, was intrigued by the rare, culturally-rich gems from less well-resourced areas – Latin America, Africa and Asia.

She recognized the struggle required to create non-fiction rooted in children's rights and needs, from producers who got rare access to a broadcaster's single camera. Ursula celebrated marvelously talented animators who worked in isolation because their national channels had no children's department. She understood the common cause among producers across a region and how bringing them together to share expertise could elevate quality children's TV.

Ursula created the PRIX JEUNESSE 'suitcase' screenings, bringing the festival's best and most intriguing programs to professional, student and youth audiences worldwide. She instituted seminars and workshops in Munich and abroad.

Ursula at PRIX JEUNESSE 2004

Most importantly, Uli championed regional gatherings that launched content and idea exchange networks, like PRIX JEUNESSE Ibero-Americano and ALA in Latin America, and the Children's Broadcasting Foundation for Africa. She strengthened the Asia-Pacific Broadcasting Union's co-productions and 'swaps', financially and by supporting expert advisors.

Ursula was 'present at the birth' – on the team that launched – PRIX JEUNESSE in 1964. Her multilingual skills, organized nature and love for the arts shaped the German festival with a French name. Simultaneously gracious and imperious, Uli ran the festival with both German precision and gemütlichkeit.

Uli with David Kleeman

"Diplomatic, elegant, generous, sometimes bossy and critical, she was dynamic and tireless. If it weren't for her, the Latin group that carries forward the quality precepts dictated by PRIX JEUNESSE would not exist. Her idea to create a Festival and Award promoting Latin American children's productions sparked so many ideas, festivals, companies and channels. Thank you Uli, you did a lot and be sure we will keep the quality flame burning."

Beth Carmona, co-founder of PRIX JEUNESSE Ibero-Americano

"Uli was a maverick who sought to make the world of children's television inclusive and connected. She championed the importance of partnerships and always created opportunities for learning and growth. She will be remembered with love for her elegance and generosity, and more for her love of putting children first."

Firdoze Bulbulia, Chair of the Children and Broadcasting Foundation for Africa

In the early 1990s, Uli was promoted to PRIX JEUNESSE Secretary General. Once holding the reins, she constantly modernized the festival and foundation, expanding eligibility, updating award categories, incorporating emerging interactive media and hosting global strategic conferences including one that sparked the launch of the World Summits on Media for Children.

On a personal note, at my first PRIX JEUNESSE in 1988, I was new to children's media. Uli took me under her wing, nurtured my passion for outstanding content and its creators and made me an ambassador, launching my career as a children's media globetrotter. I have been chair of the PRIX JEUNESSE advisory board since 2000, serving The House That Uli Built with great pride.

Ursula retired from PRIX JEUNESSE in 2005, devoting herself to golf, opera, art and travel. Ursula von Zallinger passed away in Munich on March 14, 2024, at the age of 84.

Remembered by **David Kleeman**, SVP Global Trends, Dubit

Remembering Kay Benbow

1961–2024

Former CBeebies Channel Controller Kay Benbow passed away aged 62 on 24th March this year after a short illness.

The industry reacted to the news of Kay's death with tributes across national and social media. They all spoke of her successful career, which culminated in eight outstanding years as the Channel Controller of CBeebies. There were also countless personal reminiscences, all of which described Kay as kind, caring, supportive and a wonderful leader, who always had the wellbeing of her young audience at the heart of everything she did.

Kay started her BBC career in 1985 after studying Theology at Oxford University. She worked first as a studio manager in radio, then moved to television in 1988. She met producer Ian Stubbs when they worked together in TV presentation and they married in 1991. In the same year she joined the Young Children's Department at BBC Children's as a Director and Assistant Producer.

Kay went on to work as a producer of entertainment shows for older children. She left the BBC for a while in 1999 to work as a freelance director on *Tweenies*, a Tell-Tale Production, and then returned to the BBC in 2000 as a producer, series producer and then indie exec producer.

Kay's career continued to flourish as the CBeebies channel launched in 2002. At that stage she was already showing talent for discovering talent. The tributes that have poured in mention time and again that Kay gave many people their first start. She launched the careers of Justin Fletcher and Blue Zoo Animation to name just two notables, and they are still at the top of their game.

In 2006 Kay was appointed Head of CBeebies Production, Animation and Acquisitions and she began to make many successful relationships with international partners as well as with UK companies. In 2010 she was appointed Channel Controller of CBeebies and so began the reign of "Queen Beebies" as she was affectionately known.

As Channel Controller, Kay had an unerring eye for a good show and every commission she made was successful. There are so many! But among them she commissioned animations such as *Hey Duggee*, *Bing* and *Sarah & Duck*, she commissioned *Pablo*, which brought the condition of autism to light for young audiences, she commissioned *Alphablocks* and *Numberblocks* and she commissioned the channel's first live action scripted show, *Topsy and Tim*, followed later by *Old Jack's Boat*, starring Bernard Cribbins. She also worked closely with Anne Wood from Ragdoll Productions on several shows.

One of things I'm most proud of is that together we brought the joys of live theatre to television, firstly through our partnership with the Northern Ballet, then with a series of immensely popular live Christmas shows. After that we tackled Shakespeare and instigated the *CBeebies Proms*, and children and their families loved it all.

Kay also moulded the channel to reflect the diversity of our young audience and her motto was "everyone is welcome" at CBeebies. Her channel campaigns were flawless in the clarity of their messaging. The 'learning through play' ethos was present in all her commissions and she understood the young audience like no other.

In her time as Controller, CBeebies won BAFTA Channel of the Year four times and RTS Channel of the Year in 2019. She received an Honorary Degree from Sheffield University in 2017 for services to the children's industry.

Since leaving the BBC in 2018 Kay worked as an executive consultant and script editor on several independent series, such as *Roots and Fruits* for CBeebies and *The World According to Grandpa* for Milkshake! She was also a supporter of and donor to CMF from its earliest days.

Kay was my dear friend for 33 years. We first worked together in 1991, when she returned to work after her honeymoon, and our relationship as close colleagues, allies and friends has been a joy throughout. She was kind, generous, fiercely loyal, extremely clever and absolutely passionate about the things that meant most to her – her family of course, of whom she was so proud and on whom she relied so much – they were everything to her. Passionate also about her friends, her work and Arsenal Football Club, of course. She loved gardening, the theatre, yoga, dancing – and she did enjoy a good gossip!

Kay was loved and respected in equal measure by everyone she worked with, as all the tributes to her have demonstrated so movingly. If only she could have seen the wonderful things people have written about her and understood what a difference she made to so many lives.

 Remembered by **Alison Stewart**

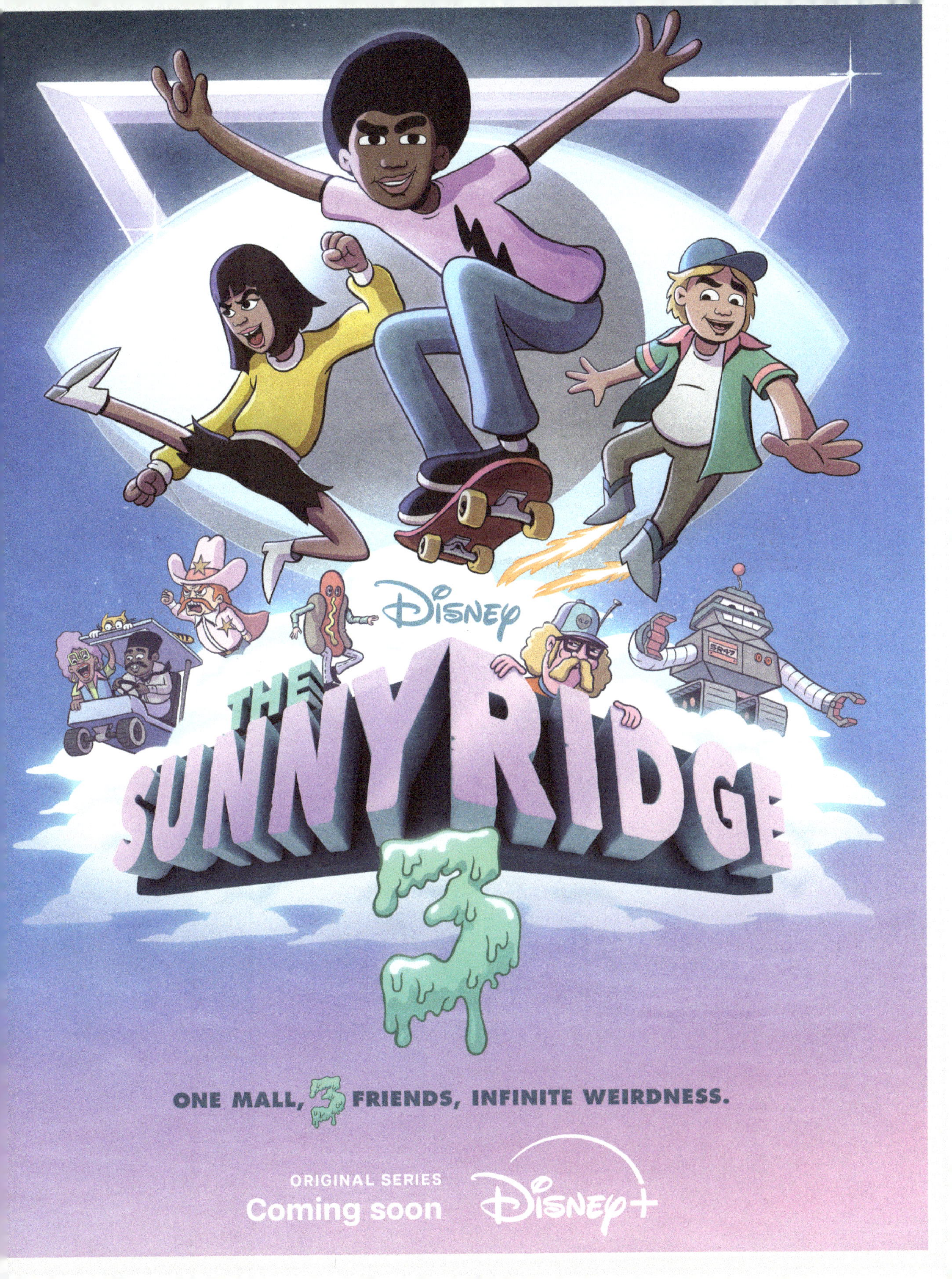
Disney
THE SUNNYRIDGE 3
SR47
ONE MALL, 3 FRIENDS, INFINITE WEIRDNESS.
ORIGINAL SERIES
Coming soon
Disney+

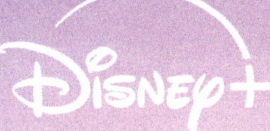

Contributors

Jamie Amor

Jaime writes and presents the *Cosmic Kids Yoga* series on YouTube and on the Cosmic Kids App. She brings a mix of Mary Poppins meets Fred Rogers meets Wonder Woman! With over 440M views on her channel and over 1.6M subscribers, Jaime has spent the past 12 years introducing kids, parents and teachers to yoga in a totally unique way by blending storytelling with yoga to make it fun and engaging for kids. Not only has *Cosmic Kids* amassed a huge following for the yoga adventures, they have also created a suite of other series to include mindfulness, meditation, sleep stories and music to create an entertaining package of high quality content to make a positive difference to kids' wellbeing worldwide. Now *Cosmic Kids* is making the leap to broadcast TV, producing an original new show for Sky Kids.

Dr Stephen Barclay

Steven is a researcher who has published on education, literacy and media policy, journalism and community regeneration. He holds a PhD in Media and Communications from the University of Westminster on the history of education and media policy. He has published on the history of school broadcasting, literacy in educational media, local media and resident perceptions of 'local news deserts', public service media policy in Europe and community regeneration policy in the UK.

Professor Rachael Bedford

Rachael Bedford BA, PhD is Professor in Biological and Experimental Psychology at Queen Mary, University of London. Her research focuses on understanding the mechanisms that drive both typical and atypical development. Her research programme aims to identify and test the impact of environmental factors, including screen time, on children's development, to build an evidence base for parents and early years practitioners and inform more personalised treatment and guidelines.

Professor Richard Berger

Richard Berger is Professor of Media & Education, in the Faculty of Media & Communication, Bournemouth University. Richard has been involved in education research for over 15 years. He has trained teachers all over the world and now supervises education doctorates. His research interests are in the marginalised voices of children and young people. He has recently worked with unaccompanied refugee youths, and he is currently working with a group of neurodiverse teenagers on a creative project. Richard is part of a large international network of EU scholars, working to transition marginalised young adults into education and work. Richard has also published extensively about adaptation and remaking culture in publications such as the Journal of Adaptation in Film & Performance. His most recent work has been published in *The Eternal Future of the 1930s* (edited by Dennis Cutchins & Dennis Perry, 2023) and *Radical Children's Film and Television* (edited by Noel Brown, 2024). Early in his career, Richard featured in 'Bogies', which has gained an 'afterlife' on Youtube.

Dr Gregory Boardman

Co-founder of production consultancy Three Stones Media, Gregory is a producer, composer, musician and writer who worked with the *Rastamouse* creators to develop the multi-award-winning television series. Having played a key role developing the groundbreaking *Apple Tree House* for CBeebies and the *Happy Dance* series for Sky Kids, Gregory is currently focusing on the development of the *Rastamouse Movie*.

In addition to his extensive experience editing scripts (*The Bill*, *Peak Practice*, *Emmerdale*) and producing for television (*As If*, *Suburban Shootout*), Gregory was instrumental in taking *Rastamouse* into live events and music education. Gregory holds a PhD in Music. Completing master's level research at UCL's Institute of Education in 2018 he has since returned to academia with a long term research project exploring young people's relationship with music and creativity in the classroom.

Dr Liam Burke

Associate Professor Liam Burke is the discipline leader of Cinema and Screen Studies at Swinburne University of Technology, Australia, where he is also a member of the Centre for Transformative Media Technologies. Liam has published widely on comic books, animation, adaptation, and media and national identity. Prior to entering academia Liam worked for several arts organisations including the Irish Film & Television Academy (IFTA). Liam is a chief investigator of the Australian Children's Television Cultures research project funded by the Australian Children's Television Foundation.

Greg Childs OBE

Greg Childs OBE is Director of the Children's Media Foundation.

Greg worked for over 25 years at the BBC, mainly as a director, producer and executive producer of children's programmes. He created the first Children's BBC websites and, as Head of Children's Digital, developed and launched the children's channels, CBBC and CBeebies. Greg left the BBC in 2004 and went on to advise producers on digital, interactive and cross-platform strategies, and broadcasters on channel launches, digital futures and operational management. He was in the launch teams for Teachers TV and the CITV Channel in the UK, and was advisor to the Al Jazeera Children's Channel for three years. He also consulted with the European Broadcasting Union on their Children's and Youth strategy.

In his role as Editorial Director of the Children's Media Conference (CMC), Greg has grown this annual event into a gathering of 1,000+ delegates, with over 200 speakers, while CMC also hosts the British delegation to the important Kidscreen market in the USA. Up to 2019, Greg also spent 15 years as one of the Heads of Study for the German Akademie für Kindermedien.

Greg was awarded an OBE in the 2022 New Year Honours List for services to exports and the children's media sector.

Dr Chris Davies

Dr Chris Davies is Compliance Manager at the British Board of Film Classification (BBFC), overseeing the classification of content being released in cinemas, on physical media (DVD/Blu-ray) and online across the UK. He also manages research projects, including the 2024 Classification Guidelines Research, and is a key liaison with the BBFC's streaming partners, including Netflix and Amazon Prime Video. He has a PhD in Film Studies from the University of Exeter and is the author of *Blockbusters and the Ancient World: Allegory and Warfare in Contemporary Hollywood* (Bloomsbury, 2019).

Jackie Edwards

Jackie is a passionate advocate for public service television and until very recently, was living her dream job as the Head of the British Film Institute's Young Audiences Content Fund, responsible for the implementation of this game-changing UK Government initiative to stimulate the provision of public service content for audiences aged 0–18.

This hugely successful three-year pilot awarded £44.1M of funding supporting 61 brand new commissions for UK children and teens and funded the development of a further 160 new projects, over 9% of which have already been commissioned. The Fund has been a powerful lever in stimulating a sector in market failure.

Jackie joined the BFI in 2019 from BBC Children's where she was the Head of Acquisitions and Independent Animation, responsible for pre-buying and acquiring live action and animated programming for CBeebies, CBBC and iPlayer. She joined the BBC in 2008 as Content Manager and Executive Producer.

Prior to the BBC Jackie was an award-winning producer in the independent sector for 14 years, developing, financing and producing specials and series for young audiences.

Claire Essex

Claire Essex BSc MSc is a PhD student at the Centre for Brain and Cognitive Development, Birkbeck, University of London. Her research focuses on examining the dynamics of attention in response to children's media to better understand how aspects of the content (ie. narrative complexity, editing techniques) influence a child's ability to comprehend and learn from the content they view. Her research uses EEG, eye-tracking and developmental measures to explore these dynamics.

Dr Ysabel Gerrard

Ysabel is a Senior Lecturer in Digital Communication at the University of Sheffield. Her research explores youth cultures and/on social media, including topics like mental health moderation, anonymous apps and bullying, and digital photo editing and body image. Ysabel's academic research has been published in journals like *New Media & Society* and the *Internet Policy Review*, and she has also written for non-academic outlets like *The Guardian* and *WIRED*. She has a forthcoming book with the University of California Press, titled *The Kids are Online: Confronting the Myths and Realities of Young Digital Life* (University of California Press, 2025), and is a member of Meta's Suicide and Self-Injury Advisory Board.

Sam Harris

Sam Harris CMRS, is Director of Auger Insights. Sam is a research expert with a decade's worth of experience helping brands understand the lives and needs of kids, teens and young adults all around the world. From focus groups to online communities and in-person shop-alongs – if you need better insights into your audience, he'd love to chat!

augerinsights.com
sam@augerinsights.com

Patricia Hidalgo

Patricia Hidalgo is Director of Children's & Education at the BBC. She is responsible for developing and implementing creative and editorial strategies for BBC Children's and BBC Education services across all platforms including BBC's iPlayer, CBeebies and CBBC, with a focus on the strategic future direction of media consumption and business models, overseeing all the division's content output including in-house productions, co-productions and acquisitions.

Patricia has a strong industry track record and is behind some of the most successful shows in kids' TV. During her last six years at Turner she was responsible for the production of the multiple award-winning series *The Amazing World Of Gumball*, as well as the Emile-awarded and BAFTA-nominated *The Heroic Adventures Of The Valiant Prince Ivandoe*. In 2017 Hidalgo was awarded World Screen's Global Kids Trendsetter award for her outstanding contribution to the kids' media industry.

Prior to her role at Turner, Patricia spent 15 years at Disney where she held a number of senior roles in Spain, Italy and the UK.

Anna Home OBE

Anna is Chair of the CMF Board and a founder Lifetime Patron of the organisation.

Anna joined BBC radio in 1960 and started in Children's Television in 1964 where she worked as a researcher, then Director, Producer and Executive Producer, latterly specialising in Children's Drama. She started *Grange Hill*, the controversial school series. From 1981–86 she worked at the ITV company TVS where she was Deputy Director of Programmes. In 1986 she returned to the BBC as Head of Children's programmes responsible for all children's output. She revived the Sunday teatime classic dramas and one of her last decisions before retiring was to commission *Teletubbies*.

After retiring from the BBC, Anna was Chief Executive of The Children's Film & Television Foundation until it merged into CMF in 2012.

Anna has won many awards including a BAFTA lifetime achievement award. She was the first chair of the BAFTA Children's Committee, has chaired both the EBU Children's and Youth Working Group and the Prix Jeunesse International Advisory Board. Anna was the Chair of the Save Kids' TV Campaign and the Showcomotion Children's Media Conference Advisory Committee.

Rebekkah Hughes

Rebekkah is Design Manager for Oriel Square, a strategy, research and publishing specialist focused on education. Rebekkah oversees the creative side of Oriel Square's design projects, including resource management, commissioning artwork, illustrators and designers, as well as fulfilling internal design needs. This is the third time she has designed the *Children's Media Yearbook*.

Jill Hurst

Having spent more than three decades working in the media sector and in higher education, Jill's first professional role as a circulation manager for an international publishing house stimulated a fascination with the behaviour of audiences. She went on to study for a BSc in social psychology before training as a print journalist with the National Council for the Training of Journalists (NCTJ). Working as a news reporter, she gained an appreciation for the value of local journalism and its essential role in engaging and connecting local communities with trusted content – particularly audiences from hard to reach and underrepresented groups.

She switched to the higher education sector in 2012, working alongside academics to maximise the impact of their research through public engagement pathways. Fascinated by how research is communicated to external audiences, Jill gained an MSc in Science Communication & Society in 2018, developing a model of practice in visual storytelling that has threaded through to her current doctoral research. Partnering with KMTV, a University of Kent owned television station, she has since created and produced more than 20 research impact documentaries and children's factual television series including *Generation Genome* and *Generation Why* – both supported by the British Film Institute's Young Audiences Content Fund and subsequently acquired by ITVX.

Hannie Kirkham

Hannie Kirkham is Research and Strategy Manager for Oriel Square, a strategy, communications and implementation specialist focused on education. Hannie leads strategy, market research and product development alongside thought leadership publications and events, and customer insights projects. She has over ten years experience in educational publishing for print and digital media in the UK and internationally, and is a primary school governor. Hannie also has an interest in the intersection between children's education and entertainment and has worked with the Children's Media Conference as Newsletter Editor, Blogger and Producer. This is her third Co-Editorship for the *Children's Media Yearbook*.

David Kleeman

Strategist, analyst, author, speaker, connector, David Kleeman has led the children's media industry in developing sustainable, child-friendly practices for more than three decades. He began this work as president of the American Center for Children and Media and is now Senior Vice President of Global Trends for Dubit, a strategy/research consultancy and games studio.

When he began this work, 'children's media' meant television. Today, he is fascinated by, and passionate about, kids' wide range of possibilities for entertainment, engagement, play and learning. David uses research, insights and experience to show that much may change, but children's developmental path and needs remain constant.

David is advisory board chair to the international children's TV festival PRIX JEUNESSE, on the board of the Children's Media Association and the Advisory Board of the Joan Ganz Cooney Center. In 2023, he was in the inaugural class of Children's and Family Emmys Silver Circle inductees, for 25+ years of service.

Sally Latham

Sally is a lecturer in philosophy with over 20 years' experience teaching A levels in Further Education. She is in her final year of a PhD in philosophy and mental health and is the recipient of the Royal Institute of Philosophy Jacobsen Studentship.

Sally has written for magazines and journals on topics in philosophy and education, including for *Philosophy Now*, *Think*, *Philosophia* and *FE News*. She regularly contributes to the *Philosophy Gets Schooled* podcast and makes zero-budget YouTube videos to help students grasp the subject. She is a contributor to *Philosophy for Children* (P4C) and produces resources for them, including on the philosophy of *Harry Potter*. She has NCTJ qualifications and a diploma in Education Writing.

Sally is an educational consultant for two childrens' philosophy TV shows currently in development. She produced the session 'Sustainability Now: A-Team for Climate Kids' for the Children's Media Conference 2024. She is a certified Cosmic Kids Yoga teacher and delivers yoga and mindfulness in primary schools, preschools and SEN settings.

Makaela Lewis

Makaela graduated from the University of Manchester with a BA in History with Sociology. She has worked at Heard for over two years – a charity that works to inspire great stories around important issues. She initially worked in the communications team before moving to the delivery team as Programme Coordinator for Heard's migration programme, Media Movers. Makaela has a particular interest in racial justice and during her time at Heard, has co-founded Heard's first space for people of colour and is leading on the intersectional arm of the migration programme – focusing on the impact of race/racism on experiences of migration.

Paul Lindley OBE

Paul is an award-winning British entrepreneur, children's campaigner and author. He founded Ella's Kitchen. Built on a core social mission, it is now the UK's largest baby food brand. In 2017 his first book: *Little Wins: The Huge Power of Thinking like a Toddler* was published, and his second, *Raising the Nation: How to Build a Better Future for Our Children (and Everyone Else)* was published in 2023.

In 2018, Paul was appointed Chair of London's Child Obesity Taskforce by Mayor of London, Sadiq Khan. In 2019 he founded Just IMAGINE If… an annual innovation competition supporting entrepreneurial ideas designed to address the UN's Sustainable Development Goals. In 2022 he was appointed Chancellor of the University of Reading. Paul is Chair of Robert F Kennedy Human Rights UK and Trustee of Sesame Workshop. Paul believes that more 'human-ness' is needed in our economy and civil society, his starting point is by working to increase the wellbeing, welfare and rights of children.

www.paullindley.uk

Ahrani Logan

Ahrani Logan is a Writer, Executive Producer and member of the CMC advisory committee. She is CEO of Peapodicity, a multi-award-winning tech company based in London and Chicago. She is co-creator of Augmented Reality brand, AugmentifyIt. She is currently writing a picture book series and creates and develops kids' IP.

peapodicity.com
ahrani@peapodicity.com

Dr Joanna McIntyre

Joanna McIntyre is a Senior Lecturer in Media Studies and the Course Director of the Bachelor of Media and Communication at Swinburne University of Technology, Australia. Joanna has published widely on the topics of Australian screen history, screen cultures, gender, celebrity, queer and trans screen representation, and Australian 'national identity'. Joanna is a chief investigator of the Australian Children's Television Cultures research project funded by the Australian Children's Television Foundation.

Professor Máire Messenger Davies

Máire is Emerita Professor of Media Studies and Policy at Ulster University. She has a BA in English from Trinity College Dublin and, after a journalistic career in local newspapers and national magazines, she obtained a PhD in psychology at the University of East London, studying how audiences learn from television. She has worked at Boston University and at the University of Pennsylvania in the USA, and later, in the School of Journalism, Media and Cultural Studies, at Cardiff University. She specialises in the study of child media audiences, and is the author of several books including *Children, Media and Culture* (McGraw Hill/Open University, 2010); *"Dear BBC": Children, Television Storytelling and the Public Sphere* (Cambridge University Press, 2001), *Television is Good for Your Kids* (Hilary Shipman, (1989, 2002) and, with Roberta Pearson, *Star Trek and American Television* (University of California Press, 2014.) She has four grown-up children, and three grandchildren. She lives with her journalist husband in Wanstead, East London. She is a Patron of the Children's Media Foundation.

Jana Navarria

Originally from Melbourne, Jana is a writer and TV script executive based in Leeds. She was a staff writer on *Neighbours* before moving to the UK and working in senior editorial roles at *Coronation Street*, *Emmerdale* and *Phoenix Rise*. She's also worked with the BBC Children's Drama commissioning team to develop UK and international shows for the 7+ audience. In 2010, Jana's debut play, *Just Another Fully Sick Asian Aussie, Mate* placed third at the Short + Sweet Theatre Festival in Melbourne and in 2024 she was selected to take part in Accelerate, a playwriting programme run by Box of Tricks Theatre in Manchester. Jana is currently working with Heard, a charity that supports the media to tell impactful stories on important issues. As the media consultant on Heard's Media Movers programme, Jana connects young people who have lived experience of migration with broadcasters, production companies, commissioners and creatives to inspire authentic stories. Coming from a culturally diverse background, Jana is passionate about giving a voice to underrepresented groups.

Karen Newell

Karen Newell is a freelance Media and Play Consultant and currently Brand Guardian for *Mixmups*, a new preschool animation now showing on Milkshake! C5. She is also co-founder and Director of ToyLikeMe, a community interest company that was set up by Rebecca

Atkinson (Exec Producer *Mixmups*) and Karen after they realised that there was really poor representation of disability across children's toys and media. Karen is also a Doubling Disability Trainer with the Creative Diversity Network, working with media companies to help double the amount of disabled talent, in front and behind the camera. After an early career in children's play Karen spent ten years at Ragdoll Productions in the Children's response team and heading up the Ragdoll Foundation.

Dr Jane O'Connor

Jane O'Connor is an Associate Professor of Childhood Studies at Birmingham City University and Deputy Director of the Centre for the Study of Practice and Culture in Education (CSPACE). Jane is an expert in child celebrities and the history of child stars. She is author of *The Cultural Significance of the Child Star* (Routledge, 2012) and co-editor of *Childhood and Celebrity* (Routledge, 2017). Jane's other research interests include children's use of digital technology, representations of children in the media and teacher educators use of digital technology. Jane is currently leading two international British Council funded projects supporting digital transformations in Vietnamese Higher Education.

Jane.O'Connor@bcu.ac.uk
@JaneOConnor100

Dr Hannah Pickard

Hannah Pickard BSc MSc PhD is a Postdoctoral Research Associate at Birkbeck, University of London. Her research focuses on better understanding how pathways of cognitive development may contribute towards the emergence of mental health problems in children with neurodevelopmental conditions. She is also interested in environmental factors, such as media use, that influence cognitive development across childhood and is passionate about working with community partners to help make research more inclusive, accessible and meaningful.

Di Redmond

Di Redmond has written scripts for most of the major broadcasters – Nickelodeon, CBBC, CBeebies, ITV, CITV, Channel 4 and Siriol TV Wales; in Europe she's been commissioned by the Disney Channel, ZDF, KIKA Germany, Universal TFI France, Content Film and TV Finland, KETNET Belgium and RSK Norway; in North America she's written for HIT NYC, the Jim Henson Company and CBC Canada.

Apart from film and television she's worked for BBC Radio, nationally and locally, and published over 100 books with most of the major publishing houses. She's written for the stage, has been a successful ghost writer and her on-going work *Bomb Girls* (a WW2 Saga series commissioned by Penguin) is rated on Amazon's top 100 bestseller list.

Steve Rock

A storytelling specialist, Steve Rock has been active in the creative industries for over 30 years, ranging from television (Children's BBC presenter and scriptwriter), to the spoken word. Steve has recently partnered with Vodacom South Africa to create a soon to be launched children's edutainment platform. Steve delivers storytelling workshops to schools, corporate clients as well as non-profit organisations. He is also a regular guest lecturer at Rutgers University, Newark, USA, on creativity and the importance of self-expression.

https://africhitv.co.za
steve@rockcreativepartnerships.com

Silvia Rusiñol Romero

Silvia Rusiñol Romero holds a degree in Audiovisual Communication and a Master's in Screenwriting, Narrative and Audiovisual Creativity from the University of Seville. She is currently pursuing a PhD in the Interuniversity Communication program at the same university, focusing her research on the analysis of children's animated television series, specifically how these narratives construct identities, values and behavior.

Dr Fiona Scott

Fiona is an internationally-recognised researcher of children's digital lives, literacies and play. She frequently collaborates with external research partners like The LEGO Foundation, XR Games and CBeebies. She is an Editor of the *Journal of Early Childhood Literacy*, a member of the Editorial Board for *Reading Research Quarterly* and a member of the Academic Advisory Board for the Children's Media Foundation. She also frequently shares expertise through invited media appearances, including national and regional television and radio (BBC News Channel, BBC Radio 5 Live) and articles aimed at public engagement (*The Conversation*).

Fiona's recently led a large-scale research project funded by The LEGO Foundation and delivered with The LEGO Group and UNICEF exploring digital play and wellbeing in the lives of 50 children and their families in the UK, South Africa, Australia and Cyprus. Fiona is now working with both UNICEF and LEGO on projects to embed research findings in the design of digital play experiences for children. Fiona is also a Lecturer in Digital Literacies in The School of Education at The University of Sheffield, where she is Director of the Literacies and Language Research Cluster.

Dr Wallis Seaton

Dr Wallis Seaton joined the British Board of Film Classification in 2019, where she works as a Senior Compliance and Education Officer. Her role involves viewing and classifying a variety of theatrical and video content according to BBFC Guidelines, relevant legislation and policies, while also helping to build on the organisation's offering to educators and young people – including working with and facilitating the programme for the BBFC Youth Panel. Wallis holds a PhD in Film Studies and her research has appeared in the edited collection, Lena Dunham's *Girls: Feminism, postfeminism, authenticity and gendered performance in contemporary television* (2017).

Laura Sinclair

Laura Sinclair is a Doctoral Researcher at Cardiff University's School of Journalism, Media and Culture researching gender representation on preschool public service broadcast television. The research is focussed on children's interaction with representation on screen and how this translates to the construction of identity and norms off screen. Laura has published research that questions the current state of representation and how young audiences experience seeing themselves on screen. Laura is an Associate Fellow of the Higher Education Academy, Guest Lecturer and is currently working on the UKRI Strength and Places Funded research and development programme, Media Cymru.

Professor Tim Smith

Tim J. Smith BSc PhD is Professor of Cognitive Data Science in the Creative Computing Institute, University of the Arts London and head of the Cognition in Naturalistic Environments (CINE) Lab. He applies empirical cognitive and developmental psychology methods to questions of media cognition and has published widely on the subject both in psychology and media journals. His research has informed media practices through collaborations with Dreamworks Animation, BBC, Channel 4, and the Academy of Motion Picture Arts and Sciences.

Chitra Soundar

Chitra Soundar is an internationally published award-winning author of over 60 books for children. Chitra regularly visits schools, libraries and presents at national and international literary festivals. She creates content for TV, stage and audio for young audiences. She is currently developing shows based on her books and original projects! She has written multiple episodes of *Nikhil and Jay* and has also written on multiple preschool shows including Audible, Netflix and Milkshake!

Chitra is also the co-founder of C3MUK, a collective for people of colour in the UK TV, film and games sector. She actively volunteers at the CMC as a session producer. She is also a member of BAFTA Connect.

Chitra has over 15 years of programme management experience in multinational corporations and fintech.

www.chitrasoundar.com

Zoë Speekenbrink

Zoë Speekenbrink is a senior programme manager at Heard, managing the Media Movers programme which brings together young people with lived experience of migration and media professionals, helping to spark nuanced, authentic stories of migration in popular culture. Zoë has 15 years experience working directly with children and young people of forced migrant backgrounds including trafficked children. She's previously run advocacy and support programmes, campaign projects and social change programmes for grassroots organisations and large not-for-profit organisations such as the British Red Cross, Save the Children UK, Barnardo's and UNICEF UK. Zoë has an in-depth knowledge of children's rights and has worked with city councils to embed these in policy, planning and decision making, centering the voices of young people in the process. At Heard, Zoë brings together her background of the migration sector and human rights based work with her interest in the power of storytelling and narrative change.

Alison Stewart

Alison has worked in children's media production for most of her career, twice at the BBC and also as a freelance Series Producer, BAFTA-nominated director and script writer, producing content for ITV, Channel 4 and Sky in the UK.

Her most recent role at the BBC was Head of CBeebies Production. Since leaving the BBC she has worked on a number of development projects as a consultant, an Executive Producer and a script writer.

Alison sits on the Board of the Children's Media Foundation and leads the CMF Executive Committee.

Chris Tichborne

Chris Tichborne is a BAFTA and EMMY winning director with over 25 years working in the stop-motion animation industry. His career started in children's TV, animating on shows such as *The Wombles*, *Postman Pat* and *Bob the Builder*. Honing his craft on these programmes led him to work on feature films such as Tim Burton's *Corpse Bride*, *Coraline* and Wes Anderson's *Fantastic Mr Fox*.

With a strong interest in storytelling through strong visual narrative, Tichborne made the transition to Director of Animation and Series Director. He has directed and co-directed a wide range of programmes including *Strange Hill High* (CITV), *Clangers* (CBeebies), *The House Trilogy* (Netflix), *The Tiny Chef Show* (Nickelodeon) and *The Sound Collector* (ITVX).

Chris also lectures in Stop Motion Animation at the School of Digital Arts, Manchester Metropolitan University.

Dr Sonia Tiwari

Dr Sonia Tiwari is a Learning Experience Designer, Researcher, Adjunct Professor and EdTech Consultant based in the San Francisco Bay Area. After starting her career in the gaming industry as a character designer, she pursued a PhD in Learning, Design and Technology focusing on children's educational media and maker activities. Her current research explores the ethical design of GenAI characters as parasocial learning experiences for children.

Dr Enrique Uribe-Jongbloed

Dr Enrique Uribe-Jongbloed is Research Associate with Media Cymru at the School of Journalism, Media and Culture, Cardiff University, and Docente Investigador at the School of Social Communication and Journalism, Universidad Externado de Colombia. Enrique has focused his research interests on cultural and creative production in Latin America, as well as in minority languages worldwide. His most recent book is *The Travels of Media and Cultural Products: Cultural Transduction* (Routledge, 2023), which presents a framework to study media flows.

Lucy Walters

Lucy is a storyteller, actor and presenter. As a storyteller, Lucy writes and performs storytelling shows supporting language development, communication, and play. Her work spans fictional and factual storytelling presenting educational content in a storytelling format. She has performed at literary festivals, museums and other live events across the UK in addition to creating and presenting content for screen.

Credits include presenting *Spot's 40th Anniversary Storytime & Playtime* for Puffin Books; *Imagine a Story* for Historic Royal Palaces Kensington; and *Post a Story* for the 70th anniversary of the Cheltenham Literature Festival. Lucy's new preschool series *Lucy's Let's Tell a Story* is currently running at The Story Museum.

Other work includes writing and touring an 'Alice's Adventures in Wonderland Learning through Stories' exhibition, presenting 'The Very Hungry Caterpillar Storytime & Craft-Along' for the Puffin Festival of Big Dreams, and 'Rosy and Fizz' – a preschool storytelling series for Bogglesox TV. As a voice actor, Lucy's experience spans animation and narration.

Professor Dawn Watkins

Dawn Watkins is Professor of Law at the University of Sheffield. She is a qualified Solicitor but left legal practice soon after qualifying to pursue a PhD in law, literature, and the visual arts. She has an enduring fascination with law and narrative, which underpins much of her research and teaching. She has been short-listed for the National Law Teacher of the Year award and is a National Teaching Fellow. In 2014–16 Dawn secured a £250,000 grant from the Economic and Social Research Council to explore children's understanding of law in their everyday lives, using a digital game 'Adventures with Lex' to gather research data. This provided the proof of concept for her current project FORTITUDE, funded by a €2 million grant from the European Research Council, which aims to improve children's legal capability through game-based learning.

Maurice Wheeler

Maurice Wheeler is CEO at We are Family in London; the world's biggest and most experienced full-service agency group that specialises in children, teens and their families

Maurice has been at the frontline of developing audience led strategies for over 25 years, working with brands in the entertainment, sports, FMCG, leisure and travel industries. He heads up We are Family's London office and as a chartered member of the Market Research Society he oversees the research and insights team who specialise in delivering insight about kids, teens and families. Maurice also leads the Global Client Services Team, guiding clients seamlessly through the entire campaign process from audience research through to creative conception and delivery of the final activation.

Maurice has won numerous awards over the years, from a Cannes Cyber Lions for his agency's work with Microsoft, through to Webbys, D&AD wood pencil and campaign effectiveness awards. Clients who have benefitted from both his professional and on-the-ground expertise include Liverpool Football Club, The Premier League, Tottenham Hotspur, Manchester City Football Clubs, BBC, Disney, Microsoft, Google, Universal Music, Unilever and LEGO.

Dr Ashley Woodfall

Ashley is an Associate Professor in Children's Media at Bournemouth University where he is Deputy Head of the Centre for Excellence in Media Practice (CEMP). With a PhD in children's media industries and audiences, his research interests span children's media experiences/culture and the children's media production landscape. Current research projects include a (British Academy funded) study into children's understanding of public service media and a (National Lottery Heritage Fund) community history project in which he is working with children as they create artwork and tell stories about their local town centre. Ashley is a member of the Executive of the Children's Media Foundation (CMF) and Co-Editor of the *Children's Media Yearbook*, as well as Editor of the *Media Education Research Journal (MERJ)*.

Ashley worked in television for many years before joining the teaching and research community, with experience that spans producing and directing factual, news, continuity, promos, commercials, entertainment and comedy – often with an interactive slant, and mostly within Children's TV. His career began within MTV and LWT's camera departments, and he still very much enjoys picking up a camera (video or stills) when the opportunity arrives. A much longer version of his co-authored article in the *Yearbook* appears in *Radical Children's Film and Television* (edited by Noel Brown, 2024, Edinburgh University Press).

Milton Keynes UK
Ingram Content Group UK Ltd.
UKHW021717270624
444731UK00005B/44